YOUR
TAROT
Your Way

About the Author

At a party someone put a tarot deck in Barbara's hands. She's held on tight ever since. Her life has been a crazy-quilt of experiences—beauty school drop-out, theatre geek, stay-at-home wife, history student, editor, academic, Catholic, fundamentalist Christian, Methodist, Nothing, Everything, pagan, shaman—and tarot helps her make sense of the eclectic soup that has been her life.

Not that she wants to make too much sense of things, at least not anymore. Not so very long ago, structure, logic, and a thirst for Absolute Truth drove her life. Now that age is mellowing her, rounding her sharp edges, she is learning to love dancing with mystery, sitting quietly in silence, and admitting that the conscious mind doesn't have to understand something for it to be valuable.

Barbara lives in St. Paul, Minnesota, with her wife Lisa and their dog, Whiskey. Every morning, she takes Whiskey for a walk and they play hide and seek with the Divine, finding magic (and burrs) everywhere. She also loves cake, art supplies, summer, traveling, and good books, a few of the things that convince Barbara that the Divine loves us and wants us to be happy.

Since her wife won't be her sugar momma, to earn her keep Barbara spends her days consulting for Llewellyn and Lo Scarabeo, creating decks, writing books, presenting at conferences, reading for clients, and teaching.

Connect with her through her website:
http://www.tarotshaman.com.

BARBARA
MOORE

YOUR
TAROT
Your
Way

Learn to Read with Any Deck

Llewellyn Publications
Woodbury, Minnesota

First Edition
Third Printing, 2018

Cover art: iStockphoto.com / 19386946 / ©Maridav
          iStockphoto.com / 65991689 / ©mashuk
          iStockphoto.com / 57477408 / ©Tatiana Karpenko
          Llewellyn Classic Tarot illustrated by Eugene Smith and used
              with permission.
Cover design: Ellen Lawson
Editing: Rosemary Wallner
Interior cards: Llewellyn Classic Tarot illustrated by Eugene Smith and used
    with permission.

Llewellyn Publications is a registered trademark of Llewellyn Worldwide Ltd.

Library of Congress Cataloging-in-Publication Data
Names: Moore, Barbara, author.
Title: Your tarot your way : learn to read with any deck / Barbara Moore.
Description: First edition. | Woodbury, Minnesota : Llewellyn Publications,
    [2016]
Identifiers: LCCN 2016042306 | LCCN 2016042380 (ebook) | ISBN 9780738749730
    (ebook) ISBN 9780738749242
Classification: LCC BF1879.T2 M6535 2016 | DDC 133.3/2424
LC record available at https://lccn.loc.gov/2016042306

Llewellyn Worldwide Ltd. does not participate in, endorse, or have any authority or responsibility concerning private business transactions between our authors and the public.
    All mail addressed to the author is forwarded but the publisher cannot, unless specifically instructed by the author, give out an address or phone number.
    Any Internet references contained in this work are current at publication time, but the publisher cannot guarantee that a specific location will continue to be maintained. Please refer to the publisher's website for links to authors' websites and other sources.

Llewellyn Publications
A Division of Llewellyn Worldwide Ltd.
2143 Wooddale Drive
Woodbury, MN 55125-2989

Other Books by Barbara Moore

What Tarot Can Do for You

The Gilded Tarot

The Mystic Faerie Tarot

The Mystic Dreamer Tarot

Shadowscapes Tarot

The Steampunk Tarot

Tarot of the Hidden Realm

Llewellyn's Classic Tarot

The Pagan Cats Tarot

The Vampires of the Eternal Night

The Book of Shadows Tarot, volumes 1 and 2

The Pagan Magical Kit

Witch Crystals

Silver Witchcraft Tarot

Cats Inspirational Oracle Cards

Enchanted Oracle

Tarot for Beginners

Tarot Spreads: Layouts and Techniques to Empower Your Readings

Contents

INTRODUCTION

Welcome to the wonderful world of tarot! I envy you this exciting beginning, this journey into the unknown. As you begin to breathe in the soul-nourishing air of symbols, unfurl your intuitive self, and summon magical insights, you will learn things about yourself and the world that you never knew before. You will discover things that you didn't expect even existed. You will experience things that, ironically, you couldn't have predicted.

It's such an honor to be your guide and introduce you to the cards that I love so dearly. *Guide* really is the best word for my role here with you. As you will see, tarot isn't as much about memorizing secret meanings as it is about uncovering the secrets of your inner landscape. No one can do that for you ... but those who've gone before you can give advice, shine a light, and point the way.

Tarot is such an incredibly apt tool for humans. One of the main ways humans understand the world is by considering things in dualities or pairs of opposites. Something you will notice about tarot right away is that this idea of opposites comes up a lot. This book's approach also uses the idea of opposites by interspersing tarot reading skill-building activities woven throughout the text.

This approach, presenting practical experience alongside information, reflects how people actually learn tarot. Plus it is more fun to play with the cards and not just read about them.

Tarot is, after all, never fully mastered. If we waited until we knew it all, we'd never shuffle the cards. So we will have recess in between lessons, although the playtimes will be more than just taking a break. In this book, they will help you form connections between the materials in the lessons and your life.

So many introductory books focus heavily on card interpretation and for good reason. The cards, like all good symbols, are layered and changeable. This is why we say tarot is never fully mastered. The cards, or the energies behind the cards, always evolve. Or perhaps it is human understanding that evolves. Probably both. Consequently, it would be so easy to write pages and pages about each individual card.

To actually become a competent reader (which is probably why you bought this kit), you have to consider so many other things than just card meanings. Your interpretations for the cards will deepen and broaden over time. Thinking that you have to learn everything about the cards will just paralyze you and for no good reason. Instead, this book focuses on a well-balanced approach to reading the cards and developing all your skills at the same time. Kind of like a well-rounded exercise program … you'll work all of your tarot muscles equally.

As you make your way through this book, you'll move both quickly and slowly. You'll jump in right away by doing your first reading at the start of chapter 1. You will see that you won't hurt or wreck anything; you can do this even if you don't know everything, or perhaps even think that you really don't know anything. You will see that you have a capacity for tapping into the wisdom of the cards. You will see that as a human, you respond to symbols just like anyone else. You will see that tarot is just really amazing. And those moments of amazing revelation, if you are anything like me, will make you want to discover more.

You'll also move slowly, or at least I hope that you will. My best suggestion, if you want to read this book quickly, is to do that ... read all the way through as quickly as you like, but then start over, reading more slowly. This will give your subconscious time to be nourished by your experiences with tarot. Give your soul time to reveal its mysteries, for as you work with these images, you will summon your soul to come dance and play with your conscious mind. When the mind and heart, the conscious and subconscious, the self and the soul weave together, that's when the real magic of divination occurs. That is what I call "being in the zone." By developing all of your tarot skills together, you will recognize what the zone feels like and you'll know how to get yourself there at will.

Are you ready? I thought so! Let's jump right in and see what wonderful things we find.

CHAPTER 1

It's All about You

The Capital T Truth

Everyone has basic questions about tarot, like "How does it work?" and "How do you know what the cards mean?" Here's where tarot gets difficult. It's not in learning to read the cards. It's in understanding how tarot works. Here's why that is the hard part: we are all looking for an answer, a clear, concise, undeniable truth answer. We think there is one universal truth behind these mysterious cards and if we can discover it, we will have access to the secrets of the Universe. We read one book that says one thing and another that says something else and we think "so and so doesn't know what he's talking about!" We get hung up on trying to figure out the Capital T Truth. Or at least, that's the way I felt when I started out. After all, if the cards are supposed to tell the future, they must have some rules for accessing that all-important information.

The Capital T Truth is this: tarot has never been absolute...not in the way it looks or in the way it has been used. But if there is no original written-by-God-and-given-to-Moses-in-stone Truth, it seems impossible to unlock the secrets that we think the cards hold. On the other hand, this realization makes everything easier. I'll tell you why soon and as the chapter title says, it is all about you. But first let me prove my point about tarot never having been absolute.

A Brief History of Tarot

Museums contain remnants of a few tarot decks made in the fifteenth century in Italy. The tarot cards that we now call the Major Arcana (in modern decks, these twenty-two cards are named and numbered) were not numbered. Tarot decks back then were handmade works of art, often full of luxurious gold leaf, and only the richest families had them. The decks were sometimes given as wedding gifts, with images of the bride and groom gracing some of the cards. The cards that we now call the Minor Arcana (in modern decks, these fifty-six cards are divided into four suits and include an ace through ten, Page, Knight, Queen, and King) had no scenes on them, just suit designators like modern playing cards (the one notable exception to this rule is the Sola Busca Tarot, which you will read about very soon).

When the printing press made printed items more affordable, the cards gained in popularity, and then lots of people played the game of tarot, also called *tarocchi*.

As is the case with games, tarot fell out of popularity for a few hundred years until the eighteenth century, when a few people found the old decks. Because the cards were full of symbols, they decided that the cards were not just a game but had deeper allegorical meanings. These people began writing books about the meanings of the cards, sometimes claiming that the meanings came from ancient Egypt. Today we have no evidence that there is a solid Egyptian connection. This doesn't mean there isn't, and it is fun to imagine wild histories about the cards. However, strictly speaking, we can't claim any Egyptian roots with any confidence.

During the Victorian era when secret societies and occultism were all the rage, people in those various secret societies used the cards to, well, hold the secrets. Some used the cards for divination while others "discovered" or referenced more "ancient" texts. Today, we believe most of these texts were invented, not discovered. During this time, one of the biggest changes in tarot occurred. A man named Arthur Waite hired an artist named Pamela Colman Smith to illustrate a tarot deck. They were both members of the Golden Dawn, one of the more popular Victorian-era secret societies. Waite didn't care much about the Minor Arcana and left a lot of the image design up to Smith. She was influenced by that Sola Busca deck mentioned earlier and, instead of using only suit designators, she painted images that reflected what the cards were said to mean.

What's really interesting is that this deck, often called the Waite-Smith Tarot (although it was originally called the Rider-Waite Tarot because Rider was the name of the company that published the deck), has come to dominate modern tarot, especially in the United States. Most tarot experts say it is the best deck with the most authentic symbols and meanings. And most tarot decks that are popular today are modeled after the Waite-Smith Tarot. In recent decades, there have been many books published about the symbols used in these particular cards, analyzing everything. For example, the number of lines forming the rays of the sun in the Sun card was thought to be meaningful, but a closer examination of the printing history shows that the number of lines changed in the earliest printings because one of the plates used to print the cards cracked, creating an extra "ray." Further, a 2015 book titled *Secrets of the Waite-Smith Tarot* by Marcus Katz and Tali Goodwin shows that many of the symbols come from somewhere other than where people had originally thought. For example, a great many symbols are from Shakespeare's writings, and some are simply from the summer cottage where Smith lived while painting the deck.

Despite the symbols not necessarily meaning what we thought or why we thought, for more than a century people have used this deck (and ones like it) to great effect. Symbols are powerful, and they get so much of their meaning from the society from which they emerge and also from the individual looking at them. Finding meaning in a symbol is a very active experience based on innate archetypal recognition, cultural environment, and personal experience. It is not necessary to go back in time to some mythical age when the cards fell to earth fully formed and with precise and unchangeable meanings. The tarot cards are sometimes called "keys." They are keys that open doors and behind those doors are worlds of meaning, some of which don't even exist until you walk through them. I think of it as being like those scientific theories that explain how the observer affects the thing that is being studied.

Other changes happened to the cards, beginning with Smith and her charming paintings. The Major Arcana cards became numbered (and the order in which these cards were numbered caused, and continues to cause, much debate among tarot experts). Images changed radically. For example, in the earliest decks, the Fool looked like a crazy person (or perhaps like a person who is mentally challenged), often with his pants falling off and his rear end (and sometimes even his genitals!) hanging out with a dog trying to bite it. Today, the Fool is shown as a pure soul about to incarnate into this plane of existence. Also, in earlier books, the meanings of the cards seemed arbitrary and didn't necessarily reflect the image on the card, which meant the image was merely decorative and not meant to be interpreted. This is very different from today, where it is almost more common to read the image rather than refer to any sort of esoteric meaning.

For a long time, tarot was used to tell fortunes. This is probably still one of the most common uses for it today, because, really, who doesn't want to know the future? However, even this has changed. Before the later twentieth century, people had a much more deterministic or fatalistic view of the world. Depending on where you were born, what class you were born to, and what gender you were, it was not too difficult to "predict" your future because it wasn't like you had a lot of choices. Today, we are more of a "you make your own future" people. We believe not just in free will but in the ability to do or achieve whatever we want. So the idea of telling the future changes, because the future is not set in stone.

Tarot is now also used for other things, such as creative writing, journaling, magical work, and brainstorming. Because of his notion of synchronicity and interest in symbols, many tarot readers are fans of Carl Jung. His work has influenced the direction of modern tarot. In fact, some psychologists incorporate tarot into their work with patients. Each year in New York, there is a conference about tarot and psychology, a clear indication of the level of interest among psychology professionals.

Besides new uses, there are more decks than ever before with all sorts of artwork and themes. Some of these break with the Waite-Smith tradition and create new ways of exploring what tarot can be. Oh, and in parts of Europe, you can still watch locals buy a pack of tarot cards at the corner tobacconist's shop and play a game with a friend at the local café.

Maybe that wasn't as brief as I led you to believe. The history of tarot is a lot longer and very interesting. If you want to know more, check out Robert Place's *The Fool's Journey: The History, Art, and Symbolism of the Tarot* or Mary K. Greer's blog at https://marygreer.wordpress.com.

I know that not everyone cares about history, and you really don't need to know the history to read the cards. It is, though, important to understand at least this very basic timeline because this is how we know that there is no full and complete Capital T Truth. This, it turns out, is actually great for you because it means becoming a reader has become easier. This means that everything about the tarot, everything about what you will do with the cards and how they will work in your hands, is determined by no one but you. Your use of the tarot cards should reflect your beliefs... about how the world works, about spiritual ideas, about what your role on this planet is, to name just a few. You might need some help in translating your beliefs into tarot principles, but I'm here to help with that. To get started, let's gather some data about you. Hurray! This is our first recess period!

Your First Reading

Even if you've done a reading before, pretend that this is your first. I would suggest doing this initial reading for yourself. Decide on a question that you'd like to ask the cards and that you think is possible for the cards to answer. Imagine what kind of possible answers you might get, what kind you would most hope for, and what kind you hope you don't get. Think about how the answers you get will help you. Especially consider how knowing a particularly unwelcome answer might affect you. Take a few minutes and write down your question, possible answers, and how the information will help you. You may find that having a notebook or, better yet, a three-ring binder will be really helpful. Throughout this book, you'll have opportunities to write down your own observations and notes. Having them all in one place will save you from having to search for them later. I like a three-ring binder because you can easily add or rearrange pages.

Shuffle the cards (however you like) and lay down three cards in a horizontal row. A row of three cards is one of the simplest and most common spreads readers use. Spreads can be a single card or five cards or even the whole deck. Sometimes (in fact, most of the time) the positions in a spread are assigned meanings, such Past, Present, or Outcome. We'll talk more about spreads later. For now, just read your three cards with no concern for positional meaning and determine the answer to your question. Don't peek at the meanings in the book!

If you feel stuck, here are some suggestions. Look at the words and numbers on the cards and see what they mean to you. Even if you don't have a set of numerological meanings at your fingertips, you probably have ideas about the difference in energy of, say, odd numbers and even numbers (for example, I think odd numbers are "spiky" and even numbers are "smooth"). Some cards have words like *Wands* or *Cups* on them. Do those words bring to mind any ideas? For me, swords are sharp and can protect or hurt; they are dangerous and take great skill and care to use effectively. Some cards, called Court cards, have words like *Page, Knight, Queen*, or *King*. What does a knight make you think of? If you're like me, you will think of quests and adventures and heroic stories. After looking at all the words and numbers, look at the pictures. Pretend that you are a five-year-old who doesn't know how to read words yet and imagine the cards are pictures in a storybook. Look at the pictures and read the story that you see. Weave the images together so that they make sense.

Write down what you did, in what order you did it, and in as much detail as you can. Even consider doing your reading out loud and recording it. Then transcribe it so you can refer to it more easily.

The more you are completely yourself, the easier all this will go. Okay, that's all for now. Off you go!

Some Answers, Some Things to Ponder

How was your first reading experience? I bet it was better than you expected, but if not, don't worry! This reading was a research expedition, not a test of your skills. Skills can be learned. We are looking for your baseline tarot beliefs. Just from that one reading and the excellent notes you made, you will learn so much about your natural tarot inclinations.

Now, take a moment to answer the six questions below. Don't worry, you won't get any answers wrong…the correct answer is always whatever is true for you. Trust me on this. Take a minute to write down your answers:

1. How does the tarot work?

2. Where did the answer come from?

3. What is the purpose of a reading?

4. What kinds of questions are good for a tarot reading?

5. How do I shuffle, select, and lay out the cards?

6. How do I interpret the cards?

We'll take the questions you've answered topically and start with a few broad ones because they may very well shape everything that follows.

How does the tarot work?

This is a big question with no one right answer. For most, the answer will be rooted in spiritual beliefs, but not always. There are some who read tarot with no particular spiritual connection (this is not to say the readers may not be spiritual, but that they don't attribute any spiritual influence to readings) but instead take a psychological approach. Although I'm using the word "spiritual" here, I'm using it broadly and including any kind of metaphysical explanation.

The psychological approach will likely involve less emphasis on prediction and more on accessing the wisdom of the subconscious mind as a way of gaining understanding about a situation. Many with a psychological approach say that it is Carl Jung's idea of synchronicity, or meaningful coincidences, that drive the process.

A spiritual approach may also have less of a focus on prediction or it may include specific predictive messages and advice, depending on what you think the goal of a reading is (more on that momentarily!). If you think you have a more spiritual approach, think about where the messages come from. Are they from a divine being and to be considered absolute? Is your role as a reader more of a channel? Are the messages from your higher self or your intuition? If you are reading for someone else, are they from that person's higher self or their intuition? Is intuition always right? Or are the messages from other types of guides or ancestors or angels?

When you were doing your reading, did you have any of these ideas in mind? Did you say a prayer or calm/ground/focus your energy in some way? If so, what do those actions say about your beliefs about a reading? Maybe for you, it is a combination of psychological and spiritual. Or something else entirely.

Nobody can say with 100 percent certainty how the tarot works. We can only say how it works for us, how it fits into our understanding of how the world works. Answering the question "How does the tarot work?" will help shape so much of your work with the tarot.

There are also those who think tarot "works" because readers "read" their clients, starting with generalizations then asking questions and watching for clues. This is called a cold reading, and I know you are not reading this book because you are interested in that process. You can learn it, but not from me. Another reason that some think tarot works is that the predictions given influence the person so that they take the actions necessary to create a self-fulfilling prophecy. I think that this can be true. I remember my days as a college tutor. With some students, I could push them simply by telling them that I knew they could do better. Mostly, then, they did, even to the point of professors checking with me to see if I had any idea why the student was suddenly doing so much better. As a reader, you have a lot of influence, which means it is very important for you to think about what you are doing and why.

Tied into this is, of course, your worldview. For example, if you think that the future is predestined, then you would naturally be confident in asking predictive questions, even far out into the future. Someone who does not believe that the future is set in any way would never ask predictive questions because that is contrary to their worldview. If you are like most people, you probably fall somewhere in the middle. I think of this as the weather-forecaster approach. That is, the future can be predicted to an extent, just as the weather can be. But the thing to keep in mind with this approach is that the further out into the future, the less accurate the prediction, and also anything can happen to change the current weather pattern. I think too many people, both readers and those who get readings, are too quick to relinquish their beliefs. It is surprising how many people say that they do not believe the future is predestined and yet expect detailed and predictive answers. This is very normal, though. Humans don't like change, generally, and we usually turn to the divinatory arts when we face uncertainty. We crave prediction then, hoping to be told that everything will be okay. We will come back to this when we explore the purpose of a reading.

Where did the answer come from?

This question is an extension of "how the tarot works." I've pulled it out as separate because I want you to really think about this. I've met so many people who get readings or even give readings without having an opinion or belief about where the answers come from. Add to this, "how do the answers come?" When you "read" the cards, what are you doing? Are you accessing divine wisdom?

If so, does it come from saying "the first thing that comes into your head?" Does it come from a careful analysis of the symbols? How trustworthy are the answers? How does your involvement as a reader and as a human (I assume you are a human … if you are a super being, my apologies!) help or hinder the quality of the answer?

Here's an example of how answering these questions will affect your tarot practice. Let's say you believe that the answers come from a divine being and that you are a channel for that wisdom. Humans have lots of prejudices and biases that we aren't even always aware of. If you are a channel, then is it your responsibility to be as clear a channel as possible? If so, what does that mean? For some, it means that as part of your spiritual practice, you include things that help keep you clear and open, whether it is meditation, chakra work, chanting, etc.

If the answers are from the divine, then that may affect how you think about the information given in a reading. Many readers spend a lot of time studying how to counsel people. It is important to think about how you will handle what you might perceive as bad news. If the information is from the divine, does that mean that you are obligated to tell the client all the information that you see? If not, how do you know which information is just for you as a reader and which information is meant for the client? Not all readers feel that they should disclose everything they see in the cards. This also ties into what kind of questions you will answer and ethics, which are discussed below.

If, for you, the answer is not from the divine but is instead a synchronistic expression of your subconscious, then what does that mean regarding the nature of the answer? Can answers from your subconscious be predictive or are they reflections of what is deeply desired and possibly not "true"?

Here is a final thing to think about, and it is something I've been struggling with recently (you never master tarot!). I happen to think that the answers come from the divine. And here's my thing. I don't think that the divine is an answer machine that pops out answers like a gumball machine. I don't know if the divine always tells us the "truth." Instead, I wonder if the divine tells us what we need to know in order to have the life experience (and learn the lessons) we are meant to learn. This is, after all, what happened in the movie *The Matrix*, when the Oracle told Neo that he wasn't the One (and we should all take our deepest spiritual teachings from movies, right?). After it became apparent that Neo was, in fact, the One, Neo tried to argue with Morpheus about it:

Neo: Morpheus. The Oracle, she told me I'm...

Morpheus: She told you exactly what you needed to hear, that's all. Neo, sooner or later you're going to realize, just as I did, there's a difference between knowing the path and walking the path.

I'm still chewing on this, though, and I hope you do, too.

What is the purpose of a reading?

The short answer to this is probably the same for everyone: to get answers! The usefulness of answers depends on the source, which is why knowing where you believe the answer comes from is important. For example, asking a five-year-old what the best snack is will probably result in a very different answer than if you asked a nutritionist. Does it make a difference if the answer comes from your subconscious, your higher self, or a divine being? In what way is it different?

Someone with a more psychological bent is probably looking for insight into how they really feel about a situation. They are looking for understanding of themselves and through that knowledge hope to figure out how to act.

When you did your reading, what were you hoping to accomplish? What sort of answer were you looking for or expecting? Were you looking for a prediction about the future, a description of the underlying energies of a situation, or advice about what to do? Were you hoping for a specific answer? Did you get it? How did that feel? Did you get something unexpected? Did you get something unwelcome? This is one thing I always tell people: don't ask if you don't want to know. By that, I mean are you really prepared for any answer? What are you hoping to do with the information? How will an unwelcome answer affect your actions or decisions?

Determining your own objectives for reading the cards will help you as you decide other things like what questions to ask and what spreads to use.

What kinds of questions are good for a tarot reading?

What kind of question did you ask? I don't just mean the subject (such as romance, job, etc.) but also what was the nature of the question? Was it a yes or no question? Was it more open ended? Did it seek information only? Did it seek advice? Was it looking for a prediction about the future? Was it about someone else? Was it about health or a legal problem?

When I was in grad school, one of my favorite professors always said that you cannot get the right answers unless you ask the right questions. I'm not sure that is absolutely always true, because I've seen instances, in both readings and research, where asking any question will get you to the answers you need. However, because a question provides the initial focus for the reading, it doesn't hurt to make your question as strong as possible. Different readers will have different advice on how to do this. It is always helpful to learn how other people do things, but unless you start from a foundation of understanding your own beliefs, you can get swept away on sheer quantity of opinions and practices.

Just from the simple act of phrasing a question, you can learn many things about your tarot belief system. As you read through this section, if upon reflection, you think, "Now that I've thought about it, I wouldn't phrase the question that way," that's okay! Part of this process is one of exploration. Don't be afraid to examine and explore. Your effort will be rewarded with clarity and confidence.

Let's start with the subject of the question. You may not be surprised to learn that for most professional readers, the most common questions are about love, money, and health. Was your question on one of these topics? Are these the sorts of questions you are most interested in? It is important to think about topics because topics lead to ethical considerations. For example, many readers will not read about health, legal, or financial issues, stating that they are not qualified to do so because they are not a doctor, lawyer, or financial advisor. These same people have no problem reading about relationships or career, even though they are not therapists or career advisors. There is, to be sure, a huge difference between "should I have this invasive operation?" and "will my ex come back?" The point remains, it is up to you to decide what line, if any, you will not cross.

Other ethical quandaries surround other topics. For example, if you are against abortion, would you read for someone wanting to know if she should have one or not? If you did, how would you keep your biases out of the reading? Or would you think that this person came to you for a reason and that reason was so you could steer her toward continuing the pregnancy? If you are against arranged marriages and a young woman comes to you for advice about accepting her parents' arrangement or leaving her family and culture, could you read for that situation objectively?

A big debate among tarot readers is whether it is okay to read about someone who isn't present or who hasn't given their permission. An example of this is if someone asks "is my ex going to come back to me?" Is it okay to read about what the ex is going to do if he hasn't given permission? Perhaps that is acceptable to you, but what if the person then wants to know if their ex is seeing someone else? This is a step removed from the person getting the reading and harder to justify, some say.

Here is a final example of an ethical "big deal" before we move on to lighter subjects. Death. Is it possible to see physical death in the cards? If so, is it ever okay to tell someone that they or someone in their life is going to die? Does it make a difference if they ask about it specifically? Most readers say, as a rule, that even the Death card (yes, there is one!) doesn't mean physical death but rather a transformation. Then they will lean in and in hushed voices tell of *this one reading* when they saw actual death in the cards. I can tell you about two of my experiences. One was a reading for a friend whose mother was very ill. She wanted to know if her mother would die soon. Turns out, she would. At the funeral, the friend threw her arms around me and thanked me because that reading led her to spend every moment she could with her mother before she died and she was grateful. Another time, I was reading at a party and someone asked about their kids (one happened to be sick quite often). I am convinced that I saw the child's death, but I did not say anything. I've never heard from the people at this party, so I don't know what happened. All I know is that I couldn't bring myself to say what I saw. Which does bring up another ethical point: as a reader, are you obliged to tell someone anything and everything you see in the reading? How do you know what to tell or not to tell? Some of these questions are so situational that you probably won't be able to say absolutely what you would do in all cases, but it is good to think about them as much as you can.

We talked a little bit about predictive readings, so we won't spend much time on that topic here, except to talk about timing and phrasing. If you incorporate some kind of prediction in your readings (whether full-out predestination predictions or weather-forecaster predictions), that will affect how you phrase questions. You will be more likely to ask "when" and "will" type questions while nonpredictive readers are more apt to use "how" questions. For most readers, tarot is not the most precise tool for timing, so I suggest that those who want to include predictions in their readings "build in" timing into the question itself. For example, instead of "will I ever find a romantic partner?" try something like "will I find a romantic partner in the next three months?" Someone who is not a fan of predictions would be more comfortable with "what can I do to find romance in the next three months?"

We'll end this section on questions with the topic of yes/no questions. Again, there are lots of differing opinions among readers. Some will never, ever answer a yes or no question. Others have no problem with it. The biggest issues with yes/no readings are that some readers are not willing to take on the responsibility of telling someone any answer so definitively (most nonpredictive readers fall into this category) and that these readings preclude the possibility that "maybe" is the answer. As for me, I find that starting with a yes/no question is a great way to establish a foundation for a reading and that, if done skillfully, can lead to a deeper examination of the situation and helpful clarity. In Chapter 8, I will share my favorite technique for answering yes/no questions.

How do I shuffle, select, and lay out the cards?

Yes, we do have to talk about this because lots of people wonder. How do you shuffle? How long or how many times? How do I know when I'm done? Do I have to cut the cards in three piles with my nondominant hand? Shuffling can become an important part of your reading practice. The repetitive act of shuffling gives you a built-in time to allow the question to unfold in your mind and focus in that moment between question and answer. It can be a really powerful, magical moment. I know of three ways to shuffle (and I'm sure there are more!) and all are perfectly fine. My favorite is the riffle shuffle, but some people don't like that because it bends the cards. The overhand shuffle is another method. After riffle shuffling, I usually end by overhand shuffling. These methods are hard to describe but you can find videos online that show them very clearly. The third method is sometimes called the mud pie method and involves putting all the cards on the table and just mixing them up, like a mud pie! I don't like this method (too messy!) and because it creates reversed cards, which I don't use. We'll get to reversed cards in chapter 3.

When you did your reading, how did you shuffle? Did you wonder about the "right way" to do it? Did you count a specific number of times (for example, seven is considered a mystical number so some people like to shuffle seven times)? If you didn't count, how did you know you were done? Did you cut the cards after shuffling? Some people like to cut the cards into two or more piles with their nondominant hand and then restack the cards in a different order based on intuition or habit.

Shuffling is more about preference than beliefs, except for this one point. If you are reading for someone else, do you let them shuffle your cards? Do you both shuffle and if so, who goes first? Or do only you shuffle your cards? How do beliefs affect these decisions? Here's how: if you believe that you are reading the other person's energy or connecting with their higher self, then you may believe that having them shuffle will put their energy into the cards and therefore into the reading. If you think that you are a channel, you may opt to have them not shuffle the cards so as not to let their energy interfere with the energy you wish to tap into. If energy is not part of your system at all—if, for example, you are more of a psychological reader—then you may wish to have them shuffle so that they feel more involved with the reading and more inclined to interact with you and the cards. Another practical consideration is that tarot cards are usually larger than regular cards and so people sometimes feel awkward shuffling them. Or they may just be nervous about getting a reading and trying to shuffle large cards adds to their anxiety. Because of this, some readers simply shuffle the cards themselves so that the person getting the reading can be as relaxed as possible.

Selecting the cards for the spread is usually done by dealing cards off the top of the deck. That is the easiest, most efficient way to do so. But for people who are very sensitive to vibrations or other intuitive sensing, there is another method. Fan the cards out, facedown, on the table, close your eyes, and run your hand over the cards until you sense which ones to select. Then either lay them out in the order selected or shuffle the selected cards and lay them out. This is another opportunity to think about your beliefs about tarot. Do you think that there are forces at play that order the cards the way they need to be ordered or do you think that individual cards will let you know they need to be picked? If you read for other people and do the fanning and selecting method, would you do the selecting or have them do it?

After shuffling and/or selecting the cards, how did you lay them out? Did you lay them facedown and flip them up one at a time or did you lay them all faceup? Laying out the cards is less connected to beliefs and more about your personal reading style. This will develop as you go along. Those who like to lay them face down and flip them one at a time enjoy the dramatic effect of flipping each card. They also find that it helps them and the person getting the reading (which, by the way, is sometimes referred to as the querent, the client, or the seeker, so from here on out, I'll use those words … see, you're already getting the jargon!) from being distracted by other cards. It's sometimes hard to focus on the Five of Cups when the Lovers is sitting right there commanding attention. Other readers prefer the cards all face up right from the start, and this is usually because their reading style includes a scanning of the cards to create a general impression of the reading before focusing on the details. This is my preferred method and I'll share with you how it works in chapter 4.

How do I interpret the cards?

When you interpreted your cards, did you most naturally connect with the images? Did the pictures reveal stories and seem to interact with each other easily in your imagination? When you looked at the cards, did you feel like your intuition (or some other part of you) almost immediately "knew" the answer? Or did the pictures leave you confused and instead the words and numbers or specific symbols in the cards (as opposed to the pictures as a whole) resonated with you?

If you responded more easily to the pictures or just felt like the answer presented itself to you as you looked at the cards, you are probably more of an intuitive reader. If you enjoyed interpreting the numbers, words, and symbols, then you are more likely an analytical reader. Earlier, I mentioned about tarot and balance. Even though you may very well favor intuition over analysis or vice versa, you will find your readings to be easier and more comprehensive when you engage both sides of your brain. The way tarot is designed and the method of reading I'll show you later will make it easy to use your whole brain (that's got to be a good thing, right?), and you will develop both aspects leading to a more balanced experience ... in tarot reading and other parts of your life as well.

Your Results

How did your reading go? How did it feel? What did you think of your answer? Will the answer help you decide about actions to take in the future? Now that you've read some more details about various topics, write out your ideas about the topics we've discussed here. Don't forget to date your notes! It's always fascinating to review your notes and see how you've changed and developed over time.

If you like things orderly or more structured, use the information you've gathered about yourself and write out a code of ethics. This will help you keep the idea of ethics in your mind as you learn more about reading the cards. As you learn more and gain experience, your ethical code may change. Or it may not. In any case, it's always helpful to know what you think! Even though it is very early in your learning, consider writing a mission statement, not for yourself as a reader (it's unfair to ask that of someone so early in their studies) but for yourself as a student. Again, knowing what you think, what you want to achieve, and how you intend to achieve it will help you stay focused.

Now that you've spent some time getting to know yourself and your own ideas, opinions, and beliefs about tarot and tarot readings, we'll shift gears and get to know your tarot deck.

CHAPTER 2

It's All about Tarot

If you found the previous chapter a little too lacking in concrete factual information, you may enjoy this one a bit more. We'll talk about the structure of a tarot deck, which is one of the things that make it a *tarot* deck. It is also one of the things that makes it easier to learn and to interpret readings. The structure is also part of the beautifully balanced tool that tarot is.

A tarot deck is a perfectly balanced oracle because its design involves both the left and the right sides of the brain. I know, I know … current research shows that the brain isn't actually divided into two halves. However, we still see that different systems or networks in the brain activate together in ways that reflect our old school left-brain/right-brain model. Perhaps we'd do better to say our "intuitive" and our "analytical" parts. Or we could say our head and our heart.

The images on the cards spark our intuition, fire up the right side of the brain, and speak the language of our heart. People who feel more intuitive often like to focus mostly on the images.

The structure of the deck, which we'll explore in a moment, engages the left side of the brain, makes our analytical side jump for joy, and allows our heads to feel very useful. People who like analyzing data and looking for patterns are usually happiest when working with the structural elements of the deck.

People are often more one or the other, intuitive or analytical. This is wonderful and viva the differences! But I think that when we involve all our parts, we create this space where things can happen … amazing, magical things … things that are much more than the sum of the two parts. When I teach workshops, I laughingly call this space the place where oracular brilliance occurs. I think it is similar to the way really creative people work. Not only does allowing both sides of the brain to play make excellent divination possible, it also makes it easier.

In our society, we value the left brain and sometimes denigrate the right brain (although that is changing). We become left-brain heavy, like someone with huge biceps and such but teeny, tiny underdeveloped legs. Then those of us who are interested in the intuitive arts often swing too far in the other direction. Our intuitive self (the right brain), which has been bottled up for so long, is so happy to finally be validated and feeling free that it kind of wants to run the show. Our left brain becomes denigrated and cast in shadow, no longer valued. Whenever anything is in shadow, it becomes problematic, popping out in inappropriate ways or at inappropriate times. Our brains are designed to work as a whole integrated organ. Both ways of looking at and thinking about the world are valuable and both actually support each other, if we allow them to.

You probably already know what side of the brain you are most comfortable working with. In your early readings, you will probably lead with your strength and that's okay! As you continue practicing with your cards, you can develop your other skills until you are nearly perfectly balanced. This evening out of your ways of viewing and thinking about the world will probably even spread into other parts of your life. Tarot has lots of benefits!

Finding Your Own Connections

Tarot is great, it's true. But what makes a tarot deck a tarot deck? You've probably seen many different kinds of decks on bookstore shelves. There are many different kinds of oracle decks, but to properly be called a tarot deck, the deck must have a specific structure. Have your deck handy, because you're going to use it soon. I know, I made you shuffle it earlier to do that reading and now I'm going to make you put it in order. Sorting cards is satisfying and relaxing, so just enjoy the experience. The first sorting you'll do is to separate the Major Arcana from the Minor Arcana. The Major Arcana are the ones with a Roman numeral on them and a name; there are twenty-two of them (the numbers only go up to XXI because the Fool is numbered 0). The remaining cards (there will be fifty-six) are the Minor Arcana. *Arcana* is a fancy word (if you consider Latin fancy) for "secrets." The Major Arcana represent important life experiences, archetypal energies at play, and sometimes forces that are outside of our control. The Minor Arcana show us everyday life situations and the various people in our lives.

Once your cards are in two piles, look at the Major Arcana cards. You don't have to put them in order at this point, but you can if you like. Flip through them, look at the images, note some of the names, and just say hello to this collection of archetypal energy. You'll get to know them all a whole lot better very soon.

Now take your pile of Minor Arcana cards and divide them into four piles: Wands, Cups, Swords, and Pentacles. You can see the names written on the cards and the suit designators worked into the images. Now take your four piles and separate each of those into two piles. In one pile are the cards with numbers (ace through ten) and the other pile has the cards with ranks on them (the ranks are Page, Knight, Queen, and King).

You now have nine piles:

Major Arcana (twenty-two cards)

Numbered Wands (ten cards)

Ranked Wands (four cards)

Numbered Cups (ten cards)

Ranked Cups (four cards)

Numbered Swords (ten cards)

Ranked Swords (four cards)

Numbered Pentacles (ten cards)

Ranked Pentacles (four cards)

Those nine piles illustrate the structure of a tarot deck. To be considered a tarot deck, a deck needs all these sections. Tarot, as I proved so beautifully in Chapter 1, is and always has been fluid. Modern decks will play with the structure, seeing how far it can be pushed before it either falls apart or is simply not useful. Some people add entire suits, some add cards here and there. Many change the names of the suits or the Majors. Some tarot purists say this is a Bad Thing. Whether you ever pursue pushing the boundaries of tarot or stay right here, that's for you to decide. Don't be afraid of new ideas in tarot, but remember to always come back to your beliefs (and we know that beliefs do change over time).

Everything in tarot is symbolic. Sometimes this makes us nervous, thinking that every symbol has a set meaning and if we haven't been taught it, we will get it wrong. We don't want to look or feel stupid, so we hold back. You don't have to. Especially not here. No one is watching; no one is judging you. Remember that symbols become symbols because "everyone" knows what they mean. Symbols also arise and gain meaning within a cultural context. The current standard in tarot (the earlier-mentioned Waite-Smith deck) was created in the Victorian era by Christian mystics, so the chances are good that you may not apply the same meaning to these symbols that the creators did. But also remember that we now know that many of the meanings we thought were intended actually weren't. Learning tarot is all about balance. You can trust your own responses to the symbols depicted and at the same time learn about some of the other ways people have interpreted those symbols. Before we talk about what other people think, let's give you a chance to see what you think.

Before looking at individual symbols in images, we'll explore the symbols that form the structure of the deck, which means we are going to focus on the Minor Arcana for a while. In the Minors, we have the symbolic systems of numbers, ranks, and suits.

If you develop a relationship with these symbolic aspects, I believe that it will make you a better reader. Part of being a good reader, of being able to combine all the parts of a reading into a coherent whole, means being more than just someone who can interpret a single card out of context. Context and relationship is everything. The cards are read in relation to each other, the spread position, and the question. This is why I think starting with the larger symbolic structures of tarot builds good reading skills.

Minor Arcana: The numbers

Let's start with numbers. As I mentioned earlier, even if you don't have (or think you have) a way of looking at numbers symbolically, you probably still have some associations. Lay out each of the suits in order, in four rows like this:

> Row 1: Wands, Ace–10
>
> Row 2: Cups, Ace–10
>
> Row 3: Swords, Ace–10
>
> Row 4: Pentacles, Ace–10

Look at the columns and think about the numbers and any associations you may have. Look at how they are expressed in the image. Consider all the aces (which are really like number ones). What kind of energy do you associate with the number one? Notice the similarities and differences in each suit. Without looking ahead or researching, just by spending time with the cards, write out your ideas of what each number could symbolize. Here's a clue: symbols hardly ever mean just one thing and sometimes they can mean opposite things! Here's an example: twos can mean union but they can also mean division. Okay, now it's your turn. Take your time and enjoy the process of exploring.

Minor Arcana: The suits

Now we will look at the suits. Each of the suits is symbolic. The Wands all have an underlying connection, as do the Cups, Swords, and Pentacles. Think about what each word means to you. It is very common to associate the four suits with the four elements. Because these correspondences may be helpful to you, I'll share them here.

Wands = Fire

Cups = Water

Swords = Air

Pentacles = Earth

It may also be helpful to know that Pentacles are sometimes called Coins and as you look at the images, you may notice a connection between Pentacles and money. I'll leave it at that so you can be free to find your own associations. Take some time now to write down in your notebook your ideas about what each suit means.

As I mentioned, many people find this connection (between suit and element) to be helpful, including myself. In fact, my understanding of the suits is a combination of the element and suit designator. I am not sure if I would have such a close connection with the suits if I didn't include the element. This doesn't mean you have to. What is most important is that you find the connection that most naturally reflects your beliefs. In case you are interested, here is a short synopsis of how I think of the suits:

Wands = the elemental power of fire and how we direct it (or how we don't direct it); we use wands to direct energy.

Cups = the elemental power of water and how we contain it (or don't contain it); cups are vessels that hold water.

Swords = the elemental power of air and how we use it (or misuse it); swords express the consequences of air.

Pentacles = the elemental power of earth and how we manage it (or mismanage it); pentacles are the manifestation of all the elements in this physical world.

Minor Arcana: Court Cards

Now take a look at the ranked cards, also known as the Court cards, within each suit. Lay out the sixteen Court cards like you did the numbered cards. Don't worry about the individual cards yet, just get used to thinking about the ranks. Using what you know (from history, from movies, from books, and from stories or myths) about kings and queens and such, look at your Court cards and write out some ideas about what they symbolize.

Major Arcana

Let's end with the big cards, the Major Arcana. These cards all have a Roman numeral and a name, as well as an image. While the Majors are part of the structure of tarot, there are no subsections here. As you begin getting acquainted with them, you can think about the numbers and the meanings you've already come up with and see how they fit in with the name and image. In addition, you can explore your own connections with the card names. What ideas does the Emperor or the Wheel of Fortune or the Lovers bring to mind? As you will probably notice, some of these cards do have connections to each other. For example, the Empress and the Emperor seem like a natural pair. Visually, the Devil connects with several of the cards, such as the Magician, the Hierophant, and the Lovers.

Lay out the cards and make note of any of these kinds of connections you notice.

What Tradition Teaches Us

Now that you've had a chance to make your own connections, let's look at some common traditional associations. You may discover that you have more in common with tradition than you thought or you may be surprised that you are a more out-of-the-box thinker. Both are great qualities for a reader to have. Being grounded in tradition helps give confidence and direction. There is power in tradition, too, because things (words, associations, symbols, for example) gain strength over time. However, anything used too often without thinking becomes stagnant and possibly irrelevant. A good reading is a combination of traditional ideas and personal insights. Below are lists of commonly used associations for the numbers, the suits, and the Court card ranks.

Numbers	Meaning
1	Seed, opportunity, gift, beginning, self, leadership
2	Balance, choice, partnership, duality
3	Communication, interaction, creation, expression, results, productivity, abundance
4	Stability, order, construction, practicality, protection, stagnation
5	Action, instability, difficulties, change, life experience, resistance, knowledge
6	Harmony, home/family, relationship, adjustment, responsibility
7	Contemplation, spirit, thought, observation, imagination, psychology, philosophy
8	Power, authority, achievement, plans in motion, action, speed
9	Completion, fullness, ripeness, intensity
10	End, finality, depletion, exhaustion, excess

Suits	Meaning
Wands	Fire, will, passion, drive, career, projects, goals, desires, active
Cups	Water, emotions, relationships, creativity, imagination, family and friends, passive/receptive
Swords	Air, intellect, thoughts, communication, truth, problems and solutions, active
Pentacles	Earth, physical world, resources and money, material life and work, health and the body, passive/receptive

In addition to the suits' meanings, there are important relationships between them. As you may imagine, for example, Wands and Cups (which are also Fire and Water) will react differently than, say, Pentacles and Cups (which are Earth and Water). The first coupling might create steam (great for romance!) or the water could extinguish the fire (too many emotional demands crushes passion). The second one could create a sloppy, muddy mess (too much emotional baggage carried into everyday life) or the water could wash away the earth (possible healing).

You will notice, also, that Wands and Swords share a common quality: active. This means that the energy of the suits is, well, active. They move faster than Cups and Pentacles, which are passive or receptive. Don't worry about understanding this completely right now. Just let the ideas sink into your mind, take root, and grow. It is enough right now to just be aware of these qualities because they will come in handy later.

Court Card Ranks	Meaning
Pages	Youth, enthusiasm, confidence issues (over or under), support, students, curiosity, skepticism, courage, fear, loyalty
Knights	Single-minded, quest-driven, focused, unpredictable, extreme, chaotic, action, power, ability, lack of deep experience or authority, energetic
Queens	Nurturer, helpful, wisdom, experience, power, deeply hidden influence, intimate connections, interested in individuals
Kings	Authority, power, responsibility, groups/organizations, mastery, expertise, accomplishment, stability

As you learn the traditional meanings, using these charts is a great way to start creating your mental map of the cards. By combining the suit with the number or rank, you can get a basic idea of the card meaning even without the image. Think about the energy of a suit and then add to that the energy of the rank or number and imagine how they work together to create a more specific meaning. For example, the Ace of Pentacles could be a well-paying job opportunity. The Two of Cups could be a decision about a relationship. The Page of Wands might be starting a new career-training course. The King of Swords could be a lawyer.

Now that you have a little more information, go through all the Minors again and combine these charts with your observations and expand your ideas. Here is something else to work on. Remember how tarot explores dualities? Part of your role as a human and as a reader is to understand these dual relationships and how they shape our experience and define our reality. Explore some of the dualities presented here and try to work out their connections. For example, how can Pages be both fear and courage? How are fives both problems and truth? Also, begin thinking about how, for example, the wild, fiery energy of Wands looks when it is in the controlled environment of the four. Recognizing and understanding these relationships are important keys to not only understanding the individual cards but also to interpreting a spread. Human brains are designed to recognize patterns and in tarot, there are plenty of patterns to see. The more you see, the more insight you will uncover in each reading.

Let's not forget the Majors. These cards are super dense with meaning, which is great and lots of fun to explore. This does, though, make it more challenging to come up with quick key phrases about their meanings. In fact, some teachers avoid doing so because they don't want their students to get stuck on these keywords. I trust that you understand that they are a beginning point only. They are useful for getting started but will be expanded upon, not only later in this book but also in your own mind. You will find that once you begin studying the cards, you will also be experiencing them in your life. You will meet them in the dreamscape of your soul. You will develop your relationship with them. Until then, allow me to share a few ideas to play with. You will notice that the keywords will include both positive and negative energies. This is because the cards don't just have one meaning but a spectrum of meanings. Some readers reserve the negative meanings for when the cards turn up in a reading reversed. Don't worry about reversed cards yet, though. We'll talk about them in the next chapter.

The Majors

The Fool: Beginnings, innocence, freedom, spontaneity, adventure, youth, idealism, faith, purity, fearlessness, carelessness, eccentricity, folly, foolishness, stupidity, negligence, distraction, naivety, recklessness, risk-taking

The Magician: Will, talent, skill, creativity, manifestation, communication, magic, action, awareness, power, resourcefulness, concentration, eloquence, trickery, manipulation, deceit, con, liar, misuse of gifts

The High Priestess: Secrets, initiation, mystery, silence, wisdom, understanding, intuition, insight, subconscious, unrevealed future, shallow knowledge, hidden agendas, inappropriate passion, conceit

The Empress: Abundance, fertility, creativity, pleasure, beauty, happiness, comfort, nature, motherhood, mother, nurturing, love, pregnancy, generosity, dependence, codependence, laziness, stagnation, smothering, stubbornness, creative block, gluttony

The Emperor: Stability, structure, power, authority, leadership, control, protection, stewardship, order, boss, fatherhood, father, ambition, reason, logic, confidence, tyranny, rigidity, inflexibility, controlling, cruelty, abuse of power, poor leadership, undisciplined

The Hierophant: Education, teaching, learning, knowledge, conformity, tradition, institutions, group identity, values, guidance, orthodoxy, rites, blessing, status quo, social conventions, fundamentalism, repression, intolerance, fear, guilt, extremism, restriction, cults, abuse of position

The Lovers: Choices, crossroads, trust, communication, relationships, partnerships, togetherness, love, affection, sexuality, harmony, engagement, attraction, duality, separation, disharmony, suspicion, jealousy, obsession, infidelity, fear of commitment, loss of love

The Chariot: Drive, ambition, control, direction, determination, success, triumph, victory, will, movement, progress, speed, travel, conquest, battle, lack of control, delay, opposition, stagnation, no direction, aggression, canceled trip, car trouble

Strength: Strength, gentleness, patience, compassion, healing, integration, courage, heart, control, discipline, fortitude, assurance, potency, virility, lust, instinct, ability, mastery, weakness, lack of discipline, control, or patience; overbearing, force, cowardice, fear, shyness

The Hermit: Solitude, introspection, philosophy, meditation, withdrawal, contemplation, wisdom, guidance, seeking, mysticism, privacy, prudence, introversion, agoraphobia, ostracism, exile, paranoia, loneliness, isolation, extreme withdrawal, self-absorption, social misfit

Wheel of Fortune: Fortune, chance, cycle of life, opportunity, destiny, fate, good luck, movement, turning point, annual event, bad luck, out of control, misfortune, failure, unexpected setback, reversal, delay

Justice: Justice, karma, cause and effect, equality, truth, responsibility, integrity, fairness, judgment, contract, legal action, lawsuit, trial, injustice, imbalance, dishonesty, hypocrisy, complications, abuse of power, red tape, bad decision

The Hanged Man: Reversal, letting go, sacrifice, suspension, surrender, withdrawal, restriction, crisis, delay, restraint, detachment, enlightenment, transformation, initiation, limbo, martyrdom, indecision, self-sabotage, narrow-minded, punishment, imprisonment, treason

Death: Death, rebirth, endings, mortality, loss, change, failure, destruction, severing ties, transitions, transformation, inexorable force, elimination, loss of hope, decay, corruption, depression, despair, inertia, holding on

Temperance: Temperance, self-control, balance, moderation, harmony, synthesis, patience, health, combination, blending, management, unification, synergy, guides, angels, imbalance, excess, temper, one-sided relationship, irreconcilable differences, short-term focus

The Devil: Bondage, obsession, materialism, temptation, shadow, fear, doubt, lies, deviancy, ignorance, sexuality, hopelessness, lack of options, trapped, scapegoat, abuse, addiction, violence, evil, weakness, detachment, breaking free, reclaiming power

The Tower: Sudden change, upheaval, adversity, downfall, destruction, catastrophe, misery, disaster, ruin, chaos, release, awakening, freedom, escape, fear of change, prolonged upheaval, obstacles, difficulties, losses, oppression, imprisonment, tyranny

The Star: Hope, faith, healing, cleansing, renewal, guidance, peace, blessing, tranquility, serenity, inspiration, optimism, happiness, promises, wishes, lack of faith, hopelessness, discouragement, feeling lost, broken dreams, dashed hopes, unfulfilled wishes, missed opportunities

The Moon: Secrets, illusion, deception, imagination, mystery, subconscious, confusion, falsehoods, cycles, bewilderment, anxiety, insecurity, dreams, nightmares, visions, psychic ability, secrets revealed, mysteries unveiled, insomnia, trouble sleeping, irrationality, shadows, danger

The Sun: Happiness, joy, fun, optimism, enthusiasm, glory, clarity, consciousness, success, celebration, energy, vitality, good fortune, greatness, life, ego, false impressions, delayed happiness, depression, burnt out, over exposure, drought, partial success, incomplete victory

Judgement: Rebirth, renewal, rite of passage, calling, vocation, awakening, change, decision, forgiveness, redemption, absolution, judgment, doubt, forsaking vocation, ignoring a calling, avoiding change, unhealed wounds, lack of forgiveness, delay

The World: Completion, success, perfection, achievement, accomplishment, victory, reward, unity, wholeness, fulfillment, endings and beginnings, celebration, center of attention, travel, delays, hesitations, false starts, stagnation, rut, incomplete work, lack of closure

Playtime

Noting your own ideas and reading about the traditional meanings is one way of getting to know the cards. This kind of introduction is a little like meeting someone online or via a résumé … you can gain a lot of information but nothing is a substitute for bona fide, one-on-one, up-close-and-personal interaction. Eventually you will spend time with each and every card. But I won't ask you to do that now (unless you want to!) because it might be too much. I don't want you to get bogged down with any one area of this book. Instead, I'll ask you to just do a few activities.

Love, Hate, Neutral

Go through your Major Arcana cards and divide them into three piles: ones you love, ones you hate, and ones you are neutral toward. Do this quickly and without a lot of analysis; just go with your first reaction. Keeping the piles separate, shuffle each one and randomly draw one card. So now you have one card from each pile. Get out your notebook, so you can write about each card. You don't have to write a lot, unless you want to, but try to write at least one paragraph. For the card you love, why do you love it? What does it seem to promise? For the card you hate, why do you hate it? Does it evoke fear or anger or something else? For the card you are neutral about, why does it seem to bore you? For all the cards, find connections in your life, past or present.

Creating Stories

One of the pitfalls of being a reader is the desire to spin the cards to mean what you want them to mean. This is easy to do because the cards do have a range of meanings and you can probably justify almost any interpretation even if deep in your gut you know you are spin doctoring. One way to guard against that is to think about cards that might show up in your reading before you do the reading. For example, if you are reading about a first date, think about what cards you would like to come up. You want them to come up for a reason … because they would represent the outcome you'd prefer. Think about cards that would be like deal-breakers. These represent things that you wouldn't like in a potential partner. If you think about them ahead of time, it's harder to twist what the cards are saying into what you want them to say. For example, if you want someone to have fun with, you might want things like the Sun (joyful) or the Three of Cups (fun loving). You would not like, for example, the Four of Cups (bored with life) or the Nine of Wands (defensive).

To practice getting used to thinking like that, think about a situation you might do a reading about. Instead of doing an actual reading, go through the cards and pick ones that you think would make an ideal answer. Then go through the cards and select ones that would be a not so ideal answer. This is a good practice to do before all your readings, at least for a while. After you've developed the habit, you will do it automatically in your head before you even lay out the cards.

Looking for Patterns

You get to do another reading for yourself! This one will use a spread with assigned positional meanings. Don't worry about "getting it right." This is not about being a smooth reader. This is exploration time. Shuffle all your cards together and ask a question about something in your life, something that is not too huge or emotionally wrought, just something that you'd like some insight about (you could use the question from the previous activity, for a nice sense of completion). Lay out six cards in the order shown below. Look for repeating patterns, symbols, and themes. You are not so much looking to interpret each card (although you certainly can), but rather to get an understanding of the energies present in the situation. Think of this as an information-gathering expedition. Don't worry about trying to figure out solutions or advice for yourself right now.

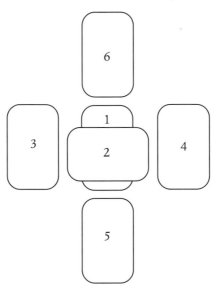

1: You.

2: The challenge in this situation.

3: The energy from the past that is affecting the present.

4: The energy in the future that can be put to use.

5: The root of the situation.

6: Your best hopes or goal in this situation.

You will look for repeating numbers, suits, symbols, and themes. You will also make connections between various positions in the spread. For example, look at the relationship between cards 1 and 2 to see how you are feeling in this situation. Look at cards 3 and 5 together to identify a fuller understanding of how the situation came to be. Look at cards 4 and 6 to see how your goals and the energy of the future align or work against each other. Try to put equal emphasis on the number and suit and rank meanings as on the images. Practice balance whether you are more naturally intuitive or analytical.

CHAPTER 3

Reversals, Significators, and Clarifiers

As you continue learning about tarot, whether you read other books, join online forums, or take classes, you will hear words such as *reversals*, *significators*, and *clarifiers*. Even though some may argue that these are more intermediate ideas, I can't send you out into the world of tarot without telling you about these concepts.

Reversals

Reversals (or reversed cards) were briefly mentioned in the last chapter, with the Major Arcana keywords. They are cards that show up upside down in a spread. See the example on the next page.

Not all readers use reversed cards. Those who do say that they add nuance and detail to their readings. Readers who do not say that they get all their nuance from surrounding cards. The best advice for new readers is to try it both ways and see what works for you. However, you know me … make sure you have clarity about your technique.

In older tarot systems, meanings for both upright and reversed cards were always provided. The curious thing about this is that so many times the reversed meaning seemed to have nothing to do with the image or even the upright meaning. Readers were required to memorize these meanings because they had no real connection to the card. Because I don't think that this disconnected approach is meaningful, I do not include rote reversed meanings in this book.

Right side up card and reversed card

Modern readers using reversals today tend to use a system instead of arbitrary interpretations. The system applies to the upright meaning and alters its meaning. Below are some examples of systems that you can experiment with. Only use one of these approaches at a time or you'll be hopelessly confused!

- All reversed cards mean the opposite of their upright meaning.
- All reversed cards indicate that the energy of that card is blocked, repressed, or denied.
- All reversed cards are read as an inner or unconscious experience.
- All reversed cards are the negative extreme of the upright meaning.
- Reversed cards mean the same as their upright meaning but are trying really hard to get your attention.

If you like seeing things from a different point of view and want to learn more about reversals, the best book you can find is Mary K. Greer's *The Complete Book of Tarot Reversals*.

You might be wondering "how do the cards even get reversed?" It's not that hard! Even for someone like me, who does not use reversals and who tries to shuffle carefully so that none occur, reversals just happen. If you really want to incorporate reversed cards, it's easy. Simply cut your deck, flip one of the sections, and shuffle. Some people only shuffle in about one-third of the cards, but don't worry about being precise because as you continue to shuffle, the ratio is going to do its own thing.

Significators

Writing about significators is always a struggle for me because it really is an antiquated practice that hardly any modern readers use anymore. However, it is a mistake to throw the baby out with the bathwater. For example, with reversals, the arbitrary meanings used in the past didn't make sense to modern readers, so they changed the approach. I think we can do the same with significators, but I fear I'm in the minority with this idea. I'll just share my ideas and you can decide for yourself.

A significator is simply a card that represents the querent (do you remember your tarot jargon?). The earliest example of this required using the Magician for a male querent and the High Priestess for a female. Well, no tarot reader these days wants to take such important cards out of the deck, so this practice fell to the wayside a long time ago.

Later practices used the Court cards. There were various methods to pick from. Some focused on astrological signs, so the fire signs (Aries, Leo, and Sagittarius) would be one of the Wands court cards, the specific card being determined by age and gender. This is not necessarily the worst idea; however, many people realize that individuals are more complex than just their sun sign. This method doesn't allow for the complexity of human nature. Other methods were based strictly on skin, hair, and eye color (coupled with age and gender). In our increasingly diverse world, this option proved ineffective. Also, there were questions such as "do you use their natural color? What if they dye their hair or wear colored contacts?" "What if they are grey or bald?" Let's not forget that skin, hair, and eye color don't even tell us anything about a person's character.

The most recent incarnation of Court card significators is basing the choice on what the person is like. Are they practical? Pick a Pentacles card. If they are outgoing, pick a Wands. Use age and gender to determine which specific card. While this practice takes in what the person thinks about themselves, it does not necessarily reflect the whole of that person. They may, in general, be practical. But what if the question is about love and in that area they are not practical at all? What if they are older (indicating a Queen or a King) but are just starting a new career and feel more like a Page?

As you can see, I have a hard time getting behind a one-card-fits-all technique. So selecting a card to be a person's significator for a particular reading can be a complicated and time-consuming task. After you've chosen the card, what do you do with it? The original intent was to set the card aside to "witness" the reading. I'm not really sure what that even means. Later, it was said to be a focal point, even though it was never really looked at and the cards in the actual spread were more of the focal point. Some spreads do have a position labeled "significator," so at least it was part of the spread.

If you are using a spread that calls for a significator or if you want to try using one, decide how you want to select it. A common way that modern readers sometimes use is to "let the deck pick." That means you shuffle your deck as usual and then just deal the significator off the top of the deck (or however you normally draw your cards) rather than going through the deck and selecting one. Another way is to think about how you feel about yourself in the situation (or how your querent feels about him- or herself) and pick a card (either a Court card or from the full deck) that represents that feeling. Then you can integrate that card into your reading. The significator card should represent your energy in that specific situation. The other cards in the reading (or at least some of the other cards) will describe the situation. Consider how the energy of your significator feels about and reacts to the energy of the situation. For example, a Page of Pentacles would feel supported and safe in the same situation that makes a Knight of Swords feel stifled and claustrophobic. Using significators in this way, to me, seems to make a lot of good sense.

Clarifiers

A clarifier or clarifying card is a card drawn to "clarify" a confusing card. What this really means is that the reader is having trouble weaving the card into the reading. In theory, this seems like a great idea. However, I'm not a huge fan of clarifiers because they can encourage a few bad habits. First, it makes readers lazy. Often, a reader pulls clarifiers because he or she either doesn't fully understand the card or can't figure out how to apply it to the specific position or situation. To counter that tendency and to overcome the actual issue, I suggest sitting with the card until you figure it out. In Chapter 8 there are some activities to do with cards that confuse or frustrate you. When you get a card in a reading that befuddles you, before drawing a clarifier, try one or more of these activities. It is better to learn more about the card rather than rely on a crutch. The second bad habit that pulling clarifiers feeds into is the desire to make a reading say what you want it to say. For example, in a reading about whether a relationship will end and the Ten of Swords comes up, it probably means that the relationship will end. However, if you want (or know your querent wants) a different answer, it would be tempting to pull a clarifier and hope that you can spin it.

Even though I am not a fan of clarifiers, I still want you to try using them. When you do, pay attention to the situation. Is it when you don't understand the card fully or when you want a different outcome than the obvious one? If not, it is very possible that you are a person who can incorporate this technique in a way that enhances your readings and that's great! Tarot reading is very personal and not all of us will do everything the same way. As long as you are conscious of what you are doing and why, embrace your personal reading style.

Playtime

Now we get to have some fun experimenting with reversals and significators.

Reversals

Let's start with reversals. You'll do several readings using the techniques listed below. Shuffle your deck so that it has reversed cards in it.

Pick a question. For these activities, I like the idea of reading for a character in a book you are currently reading or for a TV show you watch each week. That way, when you finish the book or next watch the show, you can compare the readings to what happened. If one method were more reflective of what actually happened, that would be one way to know that method is right for you.

Lay out three cards in a horizontal row and read them as Past, Present, and Future. If you don't get any reversals, keep laying cards until at least one of three is reversed.

Now for the first reading, note which card or cards were reversed and turn them upright for a moment. Do the reading as if they are all upright. Don't forget to record your readings in your notebook. You'll want to refer to them later. Then return the reversed cards back to their reversed state and do five more readings, interpreting the reversed cards in the following ways:

1. The reversed cards mean the opposite of the meaning you used for the upright reading.

2. The reversed cards indicate that the energy of that card is blocked, repressed, or denied.

3. The reversed cards represent an inner or unconscious experience.

4. The reversed cards are the negative extreme of the upright meaning.

5. The reversed cards mean the same as their upright meaning but have increased importance.

Significators

We'll use the same spread as we did in the previous chapter. You won't be asking a question, though. Instead, as you are going through your deck and making your cards all upright again, pull out your Court cards. Shuffle the rest of the deck and lay them out as below … except leave the position of card 1 empty.

Take your Court card pile and pick one card (randomly or select one that you are interested in) and place it in the card 1 position. Instead of trying to interpret the cards as a reading, look at the energy of the cards (using both your intuitive and analytical skills). How does that card feel in the situation? Then take that card out and put another one in its place. How does that change the feel of the reading? This is a great activity because it helps you practice reading cards in relation to each other and also recognizing that what might be a great situation for one person may be another person's dread.

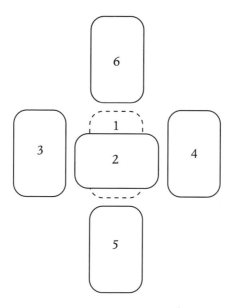

1: Significator.

2: The challenge in this situation.

3: The energy from the past that is affecting the present.

4: The energy in the future that can be put to use.

5: The root of the situation.

6: Your best hopes or goal in this situation.

CHAPTER 4

How to Do a Reading

Is it weird to explain how to do a reading before introducing the cards in detail? I don't think so. You see, a reading is so much more than simply interpreting the cards. By learning the specific card meanings first, it is easy to focus on that exclusively and miss out on learning the other skills. I can't tell you how many people contact me, saying "I know all the card meanings backward and forward (and sometimes upright and reversed), but my readings seem so disjointed. I just don't know how to tie it all together." These other skills that get skipped when we go straight to interpretations will actually make the overall interpretation easier. I call this collection of other skills "scanning" because it involves just that: scanning the cards in a reading in order to gather information. Plus, you already have a lot of knowledge about the cards just from reading and doing the activities so far.

Beginning a reading by interpreting individual cards is like putting the cart before the horse. Think of an artist creating a sketch for a painting. A sketch is a great way to get a sense of the overall composition of a piece. It is easier to see how all the parts fit together to create a meaningful and coherent whole. Scanning creates a framework and gives focus to the reading as well as provides useful information.

Scanning relies on the numbers and suits and other symbols separately from their role in shaping the cards' meanings. I'll explain the different layers of scanning in an order because otherwise it would be a chaotic mess. But you should remember that when I do a reading, I don't go through these step by step. Instead, I simply scan the cards all together and note the patterns. Until you get used to all the layers, try going through step by step, but I promise after some practice, it'll be second nature for you.

You already know how to begin a reading, so we will go directly to the scanning portion and then follow-up with some tips for ending the reading in a useful way.

Scanning

When you scan a reading, you look for patterns and connections. You also look for anything that is disproportionate. That means, for example, given that there are twenty-two Major cards, which are approximately one-third of the cards, if more than one-third of the cards in your reading are Majors, then that is something you pay attention to.

A. Look for Major Arcana Cards

These cards represent energy and events beyond your control. If there are a disproportionate number in the reading, then you have less control over events and are likely in the midst of learning an important life lesson. If there are no Majors in a reading, that means a few things: the situation isn't as dire as you think (many of us have a tendency to make mountains out of mole-hills) and that there is plenty of opportunity for you to affect the outcome.

B. Look for Court Cards

If there are a disproportionate number of Court cards (that would be about 25 percent), too many people are involved or perhaps you have identity issues regarding this situation.

Multiples of certain ranks give clues about the situation:

- Two or more Pages indicate that a willing ally or helper is near. This person may not be influential or experienced, but they are enthusiastic.

- Two or more Knights mean that there are others involved who are trying as hard (or harder) as you to achieve your goal, perhaps creating interference.

- Two or more Queens shows help and guidance from an experienced and perhaps influential person. This one can be tricky, as this person or people might be more interested in controlling than supporting.

- Two or more Kings indicate an energy similar to that of the Major Arcana cards. Someone with authority or power above your own and who is outside your sphere of influence will make decisions or take action in a way that will affect your life.

C. Analyze the Suits Present

You've already spent time working out your ideas about what the suits mean. You'll use that information here, whether you are using all your own ideas, traditional ideas, or a combination of the two.

When you scan the cards, notice if the four suits are equally represented. If not, what does that say about the situation? If many Swords are present, then perhaps you are relying too much on your intellect or the issue is one of communication. If there are lots of Cups, there is a heavy emphasis on emotions or relationships.

Don't forget the importance of what the absence of a suit might mean. For example, in a reading about a romantic relationship, you would expect to see a few Cups. If there aren't any, I would assume there is little emotional connection or intimacy.

The suits and the elemental energy they represent work another way as well. Using the suits can also help determine to what extent you can exercise control or influence in a situation. It is rare that a reading contains only one suit. Usually there are several, if not all, of the suits present. This means there is more than one type of energy present in the situation. Understanding how the elemental energies of the suits affect each other can give you an idea of the conflicts in or harmony of the situation. We did touch on this earlier and now we'll round that out. Here are how the suits affect each other:

Cards of the same element intensify each other.

• Wands (fire) and Swords (air) are active and support each other.

- Cups (water) and Pentacles (earth) are passive and support each other.

- Wands (fire) and Cups (water) are opposites and weaken each other.

- Swords (air) and Pentacles (earth) are opposites and weaken each other.

- Wands (fire) and Pentacles (earth) have little effect on each other.

- Swords (air) and Cups (water) have little effect on each other.

When an element is intensified, that is not always positive. It means that the experience is stronger or intensified, whether positive or negative.

Wands and Swords are considered active. This means the energy is active, it moves, it creates, it acts; it also indicates swift movement. That is, if this energy is present, it is moving around making things happen and happen quickly.

Cups and Pentacles are considered passive. That is, the energy is passive, it is still, it is reactive, it is shaped; it also suggests slower movement. Passive energy waits for something to happen, hence the idea of slowness, and then reacts.

When either Cups and Wands or Swords and Pentacles are present, the result is a weakening of both. They are opposites, fighting against each other, causing conflicting energy that will be evidenced in the situation.

D. Reading by the Numbers

Like Court cards, multiples of any particular number shape the theme of a reading. The numbers, remember, are on the Minor

Arcana cards as well as the Major Arcana cards. When there is more than one of any number present, these are the different energies suggested:

- Aces herald new beginnings.
- Twos indicate relationships or, more often, choices or decisions you must make.
- Threes suggest creativity, growth, and teamwork.
- Fours are a sign of stability, structure, or stagnation.
- Fives bring about conflict, loss, or chaos.
- Sixes promise plenty of communication and problem solving.
- Sevens suggest reflection and assessment.
- Eights race through with movement, speed, and power.
- Nines reflect completion and sometimes solitude.
- Tens show that something is poised to end or resolve.

Looking for multiples of numbers in your spread is one way to get a sense of timing, of where a situation is in terms of its organic evolution. Looking for timing in a reading does more than let us know when a situation might finally be resolved; it also lets us know how much control we may have to influence the final outcome.

We have some control over our lives but not total and complete control. As we've seen, Major Arcana cards and Kings, for example, indicate an emphasis on external forces controlling a situation. When a situation is in an earlier stage of development, the easier it is to change course. For example, in a relationship, if a woman has just begun dating someone, it is easier for her to break up after just a few dates. As time passes, and she and her partner start making long-term plans, like buying season tickets to a theatre or sporting event, more complicated ramifications occur if she wants to exit the relationship. If they've moved in together or merged their finances, the consequences, both material and emotional, are even larger. If it is the week before the wedding, it will take a great deal of energy to change direction. Therefore, it is useful to know how close a situation is to resolution, as that will let you know to what extent you can control or change that particular outcome.

- Multiple aces, twos, and threes mark a situation in early stages of development.
- Multiple fours, fives, and sixes are present in a situation in the middle phase of development.
- Multiple sevens, eights, and nines show up when a situation is nearing resolution.
- Multiple tens show that events are mostly finished, with just a few loose ends to wrap up.

E. Reversals

If you do not read reversed cards, simply skip this step. If you read reversals, they play a role in scanning as well as individual card meanings, just as numbers and suits do.

Regardless of how you interpret reversals with each individual card, as an energetic marker in a reading, reversals indicate a few items of note.

First, a single reversal in a reading represents an energetic block. Identify the flow of energy throughout the spread and determine how and why it is stopping at this particular point.

Second, multiple reversals, especially if the number is disproportionate to your usual number of reversals, show not just a blockage but a slump or stagnation. While a single-card blockage might easily be removed, a larger one, like a huge, immovable weather pattern, sometimes can only be endured or moved along by a lot of work.

F. Look at the visual pattern the cards make

Step back and look at your reading as one large picture. Look at the colors. What do they tell you about the situation? Look for repeated symbols and consider their significance. Squint and look at your reading as if it were an Impressionist painting. From a distance, what image emerges? This is a good time to look for energetic blockages, especially if you don't use reversals. A color or shape that stands out from the rest of the pattern bears further investigation.

Looking at your reading in this way also often triggers intuitive responses. It is a bit like yoga. After you spend time disciplining your body, your mind can achieve Zen-like states that it could not have without the physical experience. After analyzing a reading in such a systematic way, that part of your mind feels satiated and relaxes, allowing your right brain to have free rein.

Complete this part by stating aloud or in writing what you've learned about the question or situation. Really look at what you've discovered, seeing it the way an artist sees her initial sketch. Identify the structure and prepare to fill in the details.

Post-Scan

After you've scanned your spread, it's time to dig into the individual cards and wrap up the reading.

A. Read sections of the spread

Some spreads divide naturally into smaller spreads. For example, the Celtic Cross (which you can find at the end of this chapter) has several smaller spreads within it. When you get there, you'll see specific examples.

Whether or not you have a large enough spread to break into sections, the other thing to do at this point is to pay attention to how cards near each other interact. This includes noticing which directions the figures are facing or if the images blend together to create a larger image.

In this step, you are filling in broader strokes, like a color wash over a sketch.

B. Interpret each card

Work your way through each of the cards, weaving the card's meaning with the spread position and making it relevant to the question. See each card as a detail added to the sketch to create a final painting.

C. Prepare the answer

Many readers think that once they've finished these steps, they are done. However, at this point you have a ton of information and it still needs to be articulated in order to make the answer clear and complete. Review the information from the reading in a logical way—out loud or in writing. Organize your thoughts the way you'd organize any answer. Even though the detailed answer will likely be several paragraphs, at the end summarize the answer in one sentence.

This last step is, like the scanning, often overlooked. But it is always important to review, organize, and summarize the information that you worked so hard to obtain. The raw data is useful, but giving it shape helps the client more easily understand and even accept the answer.

Once you've worked with these steps for a while, I hope you will modify and tweak them to better suit your needs and beliefs.

Playtime

Try your hand at a spread that has been around since the early 1900s (although the man who invented it, Arthur Waite, claimed it was much older). Some readers simply love this spread and use it a lot or even exclusively. Other readers dislike it. You should try it yourself a number of times before you form your opinion. Not only is it a classic spread that all readers should at least be familiar with, it has enough cards to really let you practice some of the techniques you learned in this chapter. The original version of the spread includes a significator. You may handle that however you like, even if that means simply eliminating it.

As for the step in How to Do a Reading that says interpret the individual cards, you should do that, but resist the temptation to look up the book meanings! This is still your pure exploration period. Keep working on figuring out your own responses for now. Don't worry if this stresses you out. First, it means you're growing and that's good for you. It's okay to feel uncomfortable and it's okay to push yourself. Second, we'll start getting into the card interpretations in the very next chapter.

So think about a question, shuffle your cards, and give it a try!

If you are using a significator, lay that card down first. Card 1 goes on top of it (I usually only overlap it a bit, so I can actually see the significator. Card 2 is laid horizontally across the significator) and Card 1.

S: *Significator.* You (or the querent).

1: *What covers you.* This is the energy that is most influencing you in this situation.

2: *What crosses you.* This is the main challenge in the situation.

3: *What crowns you.* This is your primary goal or ideal outcome. If this cards seems negative to you or not in alignment with what you think you want, dig a little deeper, either in the card or in your own thoughts. It could be that subconsciously you don't believe it will play out the way you want.

4: *What is beneath you.* This is the foundation of the situation, the root cause.

5: *What is behind you.* This is energy from the past that is affecting the present situation.

6: *What is before you.* This is the energy that is coming into the situation.

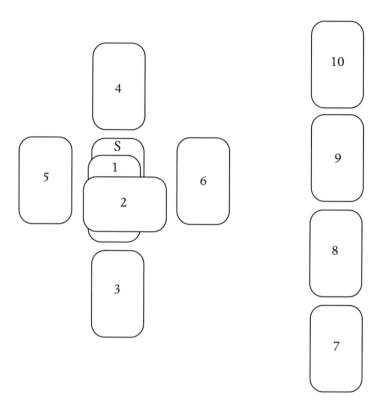

7: *You.* This card represents how you or others see you in this situation, which may not accurately reflect reality. Compare this card to the significator card if you used one.

8: *Your house.* This is the environment around you and the situation.

9: *Your hopes and fears.* This can be your hopes or your fears, but remember that sometimes these are the same thing.

10: *What will come.* This is the likely outcome of the situation unless action is taken to change the flow of events.

After you've scanned your reading, examine the smaller spreads that make up this larger spread.

The small cross in the middle is a good place to start, as it provides a nice snapshot of you in this situation. The small cross is created by the significator and cards 1 and 2.

The significator and cards 1, 2, 5, and 6 create a Past-Present-Future spread. Read these cards as a simplified version of the whole. Get a sense of the linear flow of energy before adding dimension with the rest of the cards.

The significator and cards 1, 2, 3, and 4 create a vertical line and are also a smaller spread. This one shows your motivations (card 4), your current state of being, and your aspirations (card 3).

You can move cards around, too! For example, it is interesting to put the significator card next to card 7 and explore the differences and similarities between your true self and how you see yourself (or how you are perceived). Additionally, look at cards 3, 6, and 10 together. These are all cards about the future. Don't forget to compare cards 3 and 9, too. These will reveal a lot about what you really think about the situation.

CHAPTER 5

The Minor Arcana

We are finally going to learn about the traditional meanings of the cards! Are you excited? Or did you love discovering your own connections with the cards? Whatever your reaction, I hope in the end that you smoothly blend your ideas and tradition to come up with meanings that are as unique and beautiful and as revelatory as you are!

The Aces

The aces bring new beginnings, opportunities, and gifts. If you are looking for indicators of luck or positive answers, you'll want to find aces in your reading. The only downside to these luscious cards is this: they are fleeting. Their energy reminds me of hummingbirds...beautiful, magical, and so fast that they are often gone before you realize that you saw them. If there is any ace energy coming your way, act fast or you'll have to wait until the next gift comes along.

Ace of Wands

The Ace of Wands is like being given a fully loaded magic wand. Whatever it is that you want to do, you have the energy, passion, and will to make it happen. It is a powerful thumbs-up from the Universe. It is, though, just a beginning, a spark. To keep the fire going, you'll have to feed and nurture it.

Ace of Cups

The Ace of Cups is like being given a full to overflowing chalice of magic potion. Whatever ails you, this will help. It brings healing, love, and grace. If you have some rough or raw emotional edges, let this card's waters run over you, washing away the sediment that is holding you back from loving and living with a full heart.

Ace of Swords

The Ace of Swords is like being handed a powerful weapon. Use it to cut away whatever is confusing you or blocking the truth. It sharpens your clarity and vision and encourages you to stand up for and speak your truth. Like all weapons, it can be dangerous. Truth and words can cut both ways, so wield it carefully.

Ace of Pentacles

The Ace of Pentacles is like being given a blank check. It is a seed that contains the ability to manifest your desires in your life. All the aces are lucky, but this one is the jackpot. It lets you know that if you plant this seed and tend it well, you'll find everything you need to achieve your goal.

The Twos

The twos capture a moment of tension. Things are in a delicate balance, a tight limbo. It's like the Universe is waiting, wondering "what will happen next?" Any sudden movement can upset the status quo. A decision is waiting to be made that will break that tension. Consider your options, check with your innermost self, and courageously take action. If you do not make the decision yourself, it will be made for you fairly soon.

Two of Wands

Who doesn't love choices? The problem this card shows is that neither of them are bad. That actually makes decision-making more difficult. It's easy to choose when one choice is obviously better than the other or others. When the choices are so close, you might spend too much time fretting and find that the choices have dwindled away. Wands are about your will and passion, so just pick the option that fires up your soul. This is not an intellectual choice, so you have to trust your gut.

Two of Cups

You know that moment when your eyes meet someone else's and you just know there is a connection? It doesn't have to be romantic. This instant recognition of kindred spirits happens with potential lovers, friends, or business partners. So there is this click and you have a choice. Act on it or ignore it. Take your cup and turn away and wonder for the rest of your life "what if?" Hold out your cup in friendship and open the door to a potential relationship that will change you in deep and wonderful ways.

Two of Swords

Remember that time when you knew exactly what you needed to do but didn't want to because it was scary? This is another one of those times. You know the truth in some deep recess of your soul. Maybe you don't actually consciously know all the facts and so you want to "wait and see." If you are honest with yourself, you know what's right and what's wrong. Unlike the Two of Wands with its "no wrong choices," you know what needs to be done. Doing it is necessary to your integrity, so quit waiting. It's not going to go away.

Two of Pentacles

Multitasking had its heyday but we are now aware that doing multiple things at the same time is not the best approach. Unfortunately, we live in an imperfect world and sometimes we simply have to multitask just to get through the day. You're in a serious multitasking phase. You can maintain it a while longer, but eventually something's got to give. Look at all your obligations and commitments. Prioritize them and decide which can be left undone. Do this sooner rather than later or eventually you're going to drop some balls and possibly make a really big mess.

The Threes

Threes are very satisfying to humans. Stories and jokes often employ the "rule of three," narrating through a series of three scenes or acts wherein the final one reveals the punch line or dénouement. It is a number that implies satisfaction and completion. The threes in tarot, for better or worse, bring the energy of the suits to clear conclusion. These conclusions are usually a result of the choices made in the twos.

Three of Wands

When was the last time you ordered something that would be delivered to you? Were you waiting excitedly and impatiently for it to arrive? You couldn't wait to see it and find out if the reality of it lives up to your expectations, right? That is the same energy in this card. You made decisions and took the actions necessary and now you are waiting to see the results. The lucky thing is that the awaited event is on the horizon, very nearly here. But you need to keep watching in case you have to sign for it or somehow help direct it so it arrives safely. You are kind of like a metaphorical lighthouse, drawing your desired conclusion to your doorstep.

Three of Cups

Relationships take work and attention if they are to thrive. If you've tended your most beloved relationships, there are these amazing moments when you don't have to do anything but simply love and enjoy each other. You and your loved ones are in that sweet place where you are helping each other feel like and be your best selves. These wonderful moments are spontaneous. They may feel like indulgences that you don't have time for, but really, you can't afford not to have them. They feed your soul in important ways.

Three of Swords

Truth is a wonderful thing. We would all rather live in truth than to live in a lie. But truth can be painful. The truth that someone no longer loves us. The truth that someone betrayed us. The truth that something we thought was true isn't true anymore, or perhaps never was. These experiences hurt like heck and cut into our hearts. They are, unfortunately, part of life and so there is a card to represent those truths: the Three of Swords. I'm so sorry for the hurt you are facing. The only way to get through it is to carry on. Cry, get angry, feel it. But then let it go. If you hold it in your heart, you will poison yourself.

Three of Pentacles

I love this card. When inspired creativity, a great plan, and killer skills come together, the result is amazing. Whether you are working with a group or on your own, everything needed to make something of beauty and value is right here. You accomplish things all the time but this time, this is something special. This thing, whatever you are working on, has the potential to be worth far more than the sum of its parts. Your idea will be perfectly completed and you will be quite satisfied with the results.

The Fours

Think of a square, of a four-legged table, of a box and you have a good idea of the energy of four. Sturdiness, stability, and security. Energy is contained and held for safekeeping. Like all energy, though, it has its downside. Energy is, mostly, meant to flow. When anything is held too long, it can become stagnant. Usually, the active suits (Wands and Swords) fare better than the passive suits (Cups and Pentacles) over the long term.

Four of Wands

Have you ever planned an event that turned out beautifully? If so, then you've experienced the Four of Wands. It is a more formal or planned event than the Three of Cups but with the same joy and sense of communal celebration. Also, there is usually a focus, such as a birthday, graduation, or wedding. Everyone involved gets to enjoy the excitement and fun, giving themselves over, for a time, to this temporary time out of time. The only problem is that at the end, everyone has to go back to reality and someone has to clean up.

Four of Cups

"I'm so bored!" That's what the Four of Cups tells us. You are overcome with ennui, wondering if anything good will ever happen again. When water, the element of Cups, is contained in the four, it stagnates. Sure, new life can grow in standing water, but metaphorically, it's not really the kind of life you want. The gift of this card is that the Universe is ready and willing to help you snap out of it. When you feel like this, just look around you because there is something new and fresh waiting. You simply have to rouse yourself enough to reach out and take it.

Four of Swords

Problems are part of life and we are trained by society to take action and solve problems. The trouble with that is when your thoughts are swirling around and there is no clear solution, you can make mistakes and create bigger messes. This card suggests taking a time out. Pull back, try to relax, and let the wisdom of your soul have time and space to reveal what you need to know. Any simple thing like counting to ten, meditating, or taking a nap will help more than trying to power through. The problem will still be there but you will be better able to handle it.

Four of Pentacles

Where is the line between responsible saving and obsessive hoarding? I don't know for sure but this card walks that line. Whether you see this card as positive or negative depends on the situation. Typically, energy is meant to flow and, as in the Four of Cups, these passive suits can stagnate pretty easily. However, there are times you need to conserve your resources. There are also times when you need to be more generous. Use common sense and self-reflection to determine whether you are being perfectly sensible or unnecessarily selfish.

The Fives

After the stability of the fours, the fives shake up the energy that has been resting. They are known for their chaotic nature and associated with challenges and problems. This is because they promise change and even desired or welcome change is hard on humans. Whenever things change, there is an element of the unknown and that makes us nervous. While they all represent experiences most would call unpleasant, they all also bring unique opportunities for grace.

Five of Wands

Wands represent will, creative drive, and passion. These are all excellent qualities. However, if you've ever worked with a group of highly driven and creative people, you know that clashes can occur. The gift of this card is that if you are working with a group like this or even competing with others, the environment can challenge you and bring out your best or even push you to achieve more than you imagined. The danger is that the group can devolve into fighting and posturing that can be very destructive.

Five of Cups

Loss is a part of life and there are cards in the deck that represent loss. This card is not one of them; it is a card that shows our emotional reaction to loss. This is a card of mourning and it is packed full of information. In it you see that sense of isolation you feel when you are alone with your grief. It shows also that no matter how horrible the loss, there are always other gifts that still remain. The gift is that after a time, you can cross the bridge back to your community and find healing. The danger is that you may choose to stay, alone and broken, with your grief.

Five of Swords

Ah, the card of the Pyrrhic victory, a win that comes at a price so high that it may not be worth it. Sure, you've won the battle, but at what cost? When you walk away with your bounty, what have you left behind? Your integrity? Your values? Your humanity? Friends or family? The gift of this card is that it is not too late to change the outcome. You can shift the situation from shaky win / devastating loss to win / win. The danger is that you leave essential parts of your soul on the beach to erode or wash away with the tides of time.

Five of Pentacles

Facing hunger, homelessness, or threats to your sense of security impacts your very existence and also your spiritual growth. It is really, really hard to practice love for all beings when you're in pain or hungry or scared. The gift in this card is that help is available. It is a double-edged gift: your needs can be met and the giver experiences the joy of sharing. The danger is letting your need become such a part of your identity that you cannot see or will not accept help that is offered.

The Sixes

In the aftermath of the changes brought by the fives, the sixes help create the new normal. After the dust has settled, relationships are redefined, goals reassessed, and resources reallocated. You'll see a series of unequal relationships here: people giving and people receiving. Part of the challenge with interpreting these cards is identifying which role is yours. What part do you play in rebuilding community and recreating reality?

Six of Wands

At first glance, it seems the hero is the only focal point. Someone has achieved something so wonderful that everyone wants to celebrate it. Think about some of your grand accomplishments and think about everyone who supported you as you worked toward that goal. In a way, your victory is also their victory. Yes, recognition is well deserved and you should enjoy it. But remember it is not yours alone. Remember to be gracious and generous. Share the praise and attention. It will make it even sweeter.

Six of Cups

Random acts of kindness can turn around someone's day or even their life. You never know when something you do will be just the medicine someone needs… or when someone else's act may save you. A smile, extending a common courtesy (often all too uncommon these days), or sharing a treat may not cost much but the return is incalculable. Perhaps the greatest kindness you can extend is to remember that everyone is always doing the very best that they can, even if it doesn't seem like it. This card tells you that in this case, kindness is the right response.

Six of Swords

Some changes are harder to recover from than others. The sixes are about regrouping and recreating, but if a situation has become too painful or too dangerous, the first order of business is to get to a safe haven. People in such a distressed state can rarely extricate themselves and need a hero to help them. There is no pulling yourself by your bootstraps…this is a situation that requires assistance, whether it is a shoulder to cry on or escaping immediate physical or emotional threats. If you need help, accept it. If someone else needs help, offer it.

Six of Pentacles

The most common way to obtain physical resources, at least in our culture, is to earn it. That is certainly the easiest on the ego; charity wounds pride. This card is about getting the resources you need but not through a job. Grants, scholarships, gifts, or awards are a few different ways resources are allocated. If you are on the receiving end, accept with gratitude. If you are the giver, do so with no judgment and as much graciousness as possible. When someone is in need, sometimes all they have left is their dignity. Don't take that away from them.

The Sevens

People never seem to be able to leave well enough alone. It's not our nature nor is it the nature of the world. Things always move … sometimes forward or backward, sometimes in non-linear cycles. The only constant is change. When things are good, we try to make them better. When they are bad, we want to change them. To do this, we have to assess the situation and determine what can be improved and what is the best way to go about that.

Seven of Wands

Sometimes you have the luxury of time to think about your actions. This is not one of those times. Something that you believe in is being attacked and, because the Wands are full of fast-moving energy, you need to assess the situation quickly. Is your belief worth defending and to what extent? How much are you willing to risk for your ideal? Does someone need your immediate protection? If you're all in, then dig in and prepare to fight. It won't necessarily be easy and victory isn't guaranteed. The important thing here is taking a stand.

Seven of Cups

Daydreams and possibilities are wonderful gifts. Until they're not. Too many choices can be overwhelming and lead to paralysis. Going after the big dream can bring amazing results. Some options are wishful thinking or distractions. How do you choose when all the choices speak to your heart? A little bit of faith helps, but so does bringing in some rational assessment. The options feel like they are all up in your face and you can't see past the initial glamor. Try to take a step back and get a bigger view.

Seven of Swords

This card usually leaves a bad taste in people's mouths, probably because it looks like someone is taking something that they shouldn't. There is an uncomfortable sense of sneakiness and it is hard to tell if something is being stolen or rescued. This card can represent outright thievery or misunderstood actions. It's tricky. More than anything, this card warns you about your methods, if not your goals. Even if you are only taking what is rightfully yours, reconsider your plan and try to find a way that is less morally ambiguous.

Seven of Pentacles

After you've accomplished what you want and before you gather
the harvest and enjoy the fruits of your labors, take a break. Step
back and assess the experience. What worked? What didn't? How
can you change or improve the process for next time? Did the results live up to your expectations, fall short, or exceed them? You
may be tempted to just finish up, gather your rewards, and move
on. This card lets you know that you have more to learn from
this situation. Who knows, maybe those hidden lessons are the
most important reward of all.

The Eights

Oddly enough, even though eight is two times four, it does not double the structural energy of the four. Instead it is about movement, speed, and power. This movement can go forward and normally does. However, if you turn the eight on its side, you have an infinity symbol. The speed and power no longer move forward but instead create an infinite loop that can be very problematic.

Eight of Wands

The suit of Wands embodies fast-moving energy. Add to this the speed and power of the eight, and, well, it would be best to just move aside until things play out. Whatever actions or decisions you've made recently have set in motion certain inevitable conclusions. For better or worse, things are going to click into place. If you've aimed them well, they will reach the desired destination. If not, you can try to stop them, but realize that when this many things are moving this fast, any small alteration will have magnified effects.

Eight of Cups

Have you ever been in a relationship or had a job that was just fine, maybe even good, but it didn't feel right to you? It is really hard to be in this position because it is hard to justify wanting to leave because you can't put your finger on the actual problem. The problem is that the relationship or the job (or whatever) is fine, just not fine for you. It takes a lot of courage and determination to leave something that is fine. But if your soul is urging you onward, you will continue to feel restless and maybe become resentful unless you leave and begin a new journey.

Eight of Swords

Who hasn't felt like they were out of options? Or talked with a friend with a problem and that friend had sixteen excuses for every solution you put forward? Thoughts become your jailor. When you get stuck in a rut or a terrible situation, the means of escape is not always obvious. You just see roadblocks everywhere you turn. Then you get used to seeing just roadblocks. You get so used to seeing why solutions won't work that you come to believe there is no way out. This situation is not hopeless, but first you have to figure out how to remove that blindfold.

Eight of Pentacles

Anything worth doing is worth doing well. The movement here is from acceptable to exquisite. The skills have been learned; now it is time to master them. Determination is required because, as sometimes happens with the fast number energy mingling with a passive suit, things can get bogged down. If you keep the momentum going, keep pushing yourself even if you are tired, you will be rewarded. Don't give up. Don't accept "good enough." This is an opportunity to really master something.

The Nines

You will notice that all the nines show a solitary figure. It's as if the energy of the Hermit, also numbered nine, has trickled down through to these cards. Just as the Hermit (whom you will learn more about later) has to find his own inner truth, so do these characters. Through their own particular and specific experiences, they will discover something important about themselves, and when these cards come up for you, expect the same. A journey of self-discovery!

Nine of Wands

Remember the fight that started in the Seven of Wands? This card is what happens after the battle. You've been battered and hurt, bruised and broken, but you're still standing, ready for the next onslaught. Recent experiences have taught you to be wary, to be on the defensive. There is always that line, though, between hyper-vigilance that distorts reality and sees danger in everything and sensible caution and awareness. Let the battles hone your skills. Be more sensitive to your environment but don't close yourself off.

Nine of Cups

Back in the old days, readers would tell you to make a wish before starting the reading. If the Nine of Cups showed up, they would say your wish would be granted. While we don't usually interpret this card like that now (although there is nothing saying you can't), we do carry that emotional sense of deep satisfaction into the modern meaning. You know those moments where everything feels good and full but not too full, where you're happy and in the moment? Did you like it? Good, because that's what this card brings!

Nine of Swords

This card plays out in different ways. For example, you are fretting about something before bed. You try to sleep but that wretched hamster in your mind keeps spinning ever more dire scenarios. Or, you wake up in the middle of the night and suddenly every mistake you've ever made parades across your mind, blowing you raspberries, taunting you with their perfect misery. There is usually a hamster in this scenario, too. The good news is that usually these worries are not as bad as you think they are. The bad news is that it's really, really hard to evict that hamster.

Nine of Pentacles

This is a very popular card and with good reason. It represents accomplishment, achievement, success, prosperity, and self-determination. Not only do you have it all, you also have the very particular feeling of having earned it, having made it all happen by yourself. It wasn't necessarily easy and took loads of discipline and focus, skill and plain old hard work. But it's yours and it's perfect. The only thing missing here is someone to share it with. You don't have to share, but if you want to, it won't be difficult to find a willing companion.

The Tens

The tens show endings and the fulfillment of the promises of the aces. Some say the tens are about excess, but I don't agree. Too much emotion, for example, would not be expressed as the happy image of the Ten of Cups. Rather, they show how the energy of the suits reacts with the fullness of the energy of ten. The result here is the opposite of the fours: the passive suits are happier when full while the active suits become overwhelming. Pop quiz: do you remember which are passive and which are active?

Ten of Wands

The Ace of Wands gave you a fully loaded magic wand and the advice: make sure you can feed whatever you create. According to this card, it looks like a case of someone's eyes being bigger than their stomach. Having lots of great opportunities (or perhaps obligations that are not so great) can be as bad as having none. The result is often the same: pedaling really fast but not getting anywhere. If you want the situation to change, you've got to prioritize and let go of some things.

Ten of Cups

The Ace of Cups gave you a chalice of magic potion and it looks like you used it well. Multiple emotionally satisfying relationships, a sense of emotional safety, and overall well-being prevail. Love is all you need … or at least that's how it feels right now. Your world, your happiness right now is made up of the sweet connections you've nurtured with others in your life. You are able to fully enjoy them because you've also healed some of your own emotional wounds and learned to love yourself.

Ten of Swords

The Ace of Swords gave you a powerful weapon and a warning to use it carefully. Looks like you became so enchanted with this incredible weapon that you find yourself in a bit of a mess. Whether you are killing yourself with crazy self-talk or arguing with someone who is either more skilled or simply more determined than you, there is no winning here. It would be wiser to let it go and start over. In fact, the light in this card is both a sunset and a sunrise, illustrating another aspect of the tens: they are both endings and new beginnings.

Ten of Pentacles

The Ace of Pentacles gave you a blank check or a seed of opportunity, at least metaphorically. You've planted the seed and tended it well and now it has blossomed into something with both depth and even more potential. This is not just having enough; it's about being prosperous. What's extra special about this card is that even though there is a focus on material wealth, there is also an honoring of the sacred in everyday life. Right now, life is particularly good, in part because you have people to share it with.

Playtime

These activities are designed to help you start connecting the cards with real life experiences. You will be selecting individual cards or groups of two or more cards to illustrate events in your day. If one card is sufficient, that's great. If not, if you need two or more cards to illustrate any one event in the day, use them! This will help you to interpret your readings more specifically and develop your own personal connections with individual cards and interactions between pairs or groups of cards.

How Was Your Day?

The Minor Arcana cards show us everyday life situations. Think about your day yesterday, then go through your Minor Arcana cards and select ones that create a visual timeline of your day.

Your Daily Planner and Evaluation

Think about your plans for your day tomorrow. Go through your Minor Arcana cards and select ones that illustrate how you hope your day will go. At the end of the day, select cards that illustrate how your day actually went.

CHAPTER 6

The Court Cards

The Court cards represent people. Mostly. And because of that, they can be complicated. Not so much complicated to understand as complicated to know when to interpret them as the querent or as another person. To interpret the Court cards, you will rely on, first, understanding them and then on both context and intuition. In the pages that follow, I will tell you what I think these cards mean. Here I will tell you that sometimes I ignore all that because I *know* that the Queen of Wands represents my client's Uncle Hank (physical gender is irrelevant in tarot … it's all metaphor).

With the Court cards, it is easier to understand the ranks and suits, which come together to create individual Court cards, rather than start with individual card meanings. Once you understand these general principles, you will find it easier to differentiate the Court cards.

Gender in tarot is symbolic. Kings and Knights are portrayed as male not because they only represent men but because they represent the active energy connected with the card. Queens are shown as female not because they only represent women but because the cards' energy is passive. Pages are usually shown as young people who are either male or androgynous because the energy is still in a formative stage. In the interpretations below I will use gendered pronouns for simplicity, but please, please remember that Kings can represent women and Queens can be men.

The reason other people show up in readings is because they are involved with the situation being asked about. They play an important part or they wouldn't have shown up in the reading. So your job is to figure out what role they play and how you can work with or influence them. Situations involving others can be unpredictable, since we cannot control their decisions or actions. However, by understanding what drives them, you can find ways to work with them, eliminate friction, and focus on common goals or agree on mutually beneficial courses of action.

The suit of Wands includes personality traits such as charisma, energy, optimism, charm, leadership, and warmth. Wands people are usually driven and passionate. They can also be self-focused or even self-centered. They are volatile personalities that may become angry in a flash, making them rash, immature, or cruel.

The Cups personalities are often creative, empathetic, sympathetic, nurturing, sensitive, loving, intuitive, and caring. They are emotional and value relationships. They can also be needy, demanding a lot of attention from others in their lives, as well as being overly sensitive and easily hurt.

Logic rules the Swords cards, and these Court card personalities love solving problems and making plans. They are often precise, witty, clever, intelligent, and excellent communicators. Sometimes they appear as cold-hearted and distant. Because they are so discerning, they are quick to pick up on weaknesses and can be known for their sharp tongues and cutting words.

Pentacles people are practical, loyal, and stable. They tend to value money, resources, and creature comforts. Luckily, they are also often good managers of such things. Because of their connection with the physical world, they can seem shallow. In addition, their precise accounting can lead to pettiness and their stability can turn into dullness or stagnation.

As you see, each suit has its own style and nature. If you put any three Court cards in the same situation (or in the same spread), they will all react differently and thus produce a different outcome. Below are some examples.

- All the Court cards can be helpful in a crisis. Wands will take immediate action, Cups will provide emotional support, Swords will develop the best plan, and Pentacles will carry out the plan.

- All can be good friends, in their own way. Wands will be your go-to for a good time, Cups will be your shoulder to cry on, Swords will help rewrite your résumé or plan a vacation, Pentacles will go shopping or help with your budget.

- Like the real people they represent, they can also be manipulative, with Wands daring you, Cups dumping guilt, Swords wielding logic, and Pentacles tempting you.

- All can be obsessive, with Wands worrying about their ego, Cups feeding their emotions until they block out all else, Swords will argue themselves into an ulcer, and Pentacles will fret about pennies.

It is helpful to understand their personalities because understanding what motivates people will help you move through the world with greater ease and control.

The suits determine personality but the roles played are determined largely by rank: Page, Knight, Queen, or King. The rank also determines the extent of influence the person has on the situation. Even if you don't think you know much about kings and queens and maybe even feel like such an archaic hierarchy has no place in our modern world, you will find that as symbols, these actually work really well. I've described the roles of each rank in the following pages.

The Pages

Pages are young, either chronologically or in terms of the situation. For example, they could be a teenager going away from home for an extended period for the first time or they could be a retired person going to college for the first time. They are usually enthusiastic about learning or doing something new but are probably also nervous, because they are unsure of themselves. Pages don't have much authority or influence. They usually play a supporting role. They are generally willing and eager to be included in projects. They are willing to help because above all they want to feel included. All the Pages share curiosity, skepticism, courage, and fear. They all may feel slightly off-balance and grateful for support or guidance. In exchange, they can offer loyalty and enthusiasm.

Page of Wands

This guy appears brash and bold and confident, but be careful: his ego is super fragile. His biggest fear is looking ridiculous. He's kind of like a bomb with a defective timer. Unpredictable. If he gets bored, he gets edgy and that's dangerous. He needs help curbing his dependence on external validation, his anger, his frustration … in short, his temper tantrums. Give him the opportunity to explore, grow, and shine, and he'll be an energetic friend and supporter.

Page of Cups

The Page of Cups takes himself very seriously. When he commits to something, he is all in and all earnestness. Guide him gently, helping him protect his heart without becoming cynical. Immaturity, unrealistic expectations, over-sensitivity, and a tendency toward secretiveness can make him hard to deal with. Help him navigate those choppy waters and you will win a sweet and devoted friend.

Page of Swords

The Page of Swords is smart and knows it. What he doesn't know is that he lacks finesse and sometimes wields that sword like a club. He has a deep love of truth and justice and a tendency to oversimplify complex situations. He is kind of judgy (a shadow side of discernment) and can be a gossip. Help him most by showing him how to navigate shades of grey while maintaining ideals and you'll have a great out-of-the-box thinker in your corner.

Page of Pentacles

The Page of Pentacles loves things! He can be a great collector (or hoarder). He can be very efficient (or lazy). He can be fiscally motivated (or greedy). His relationship to the material world is a work in progress. Help him to see the magic under the material and that all consequences aren't necessary physical. Guide him toward a more balanced view of life and you'll have a devoted go-to person you can always count on.

The Knights

Knights are among the most volatile of the Court cards, often unpredictable, extreme, and chaotic. They are all about taking action. They can be single-minded and incredibly focused, always on whatever quest that has captured their attention. Knights are usually more interested in their own lives than anyone else's. But they do have some power and ability, if not much experience or true authority. Whatever action they take will have an effect, for good or ill. They are hard to control, especially when focused on their own pursuits. However, if you can capture their attention and convince them to do what you want them to, you will have your hands full with a lot of powerful energy.

Knight of Wands

This knight is driven by will and passion. He wants his own way and will stop at nothing until he gets it. Or until he is distracted by the next awesome idea. He will pretty much ignore any damage he does to property or people while on his quest. The good news is that such intensity cannot last long. If you can catch his fickle attention and direct it how you want, do it quickly before it dissipates. If you cannot capture his attention, just get out of the way until he wears himself out.

Knight of Cups

This romantic dreamer is motivated by emotion and often says that he must follow his heart. Confusing emotions with soul, he thinks that every feeling is a message from his soul and worthy of acting on, and damn the consequences. He is not as actively dangerous as the Knight of Wands. Instead, his damage may be caused by neglecting other parts of his life that are equally important, only he doesn't see it that way. This knight could be hard to sway unless you lead with something that engages him on an emotional level. Logic or bottom line results will not affect him.

Knight of Swords

Here we have a thinker who is enchanted with his own mind. He feels very clear on his decision or belief system or whatever worldview is driving him right now. He has also convinced himself that his truth is right for everyone and will use his formidable logic, skillful argumentation, and cherry-picked evidence to convince the world. He flashes around wielding dangerous things and therefore can cause a lot of damage very quickly. For while he is completely committed to an ideal, he lacks strategy. Show him how your strategy can further his agenda and you can get him on your team, which is safer than the alternative.

Knight of Pentacles

The guy loves anything to do with increasing resources and ef-
ficiencies. His weakness is caution, because he fears risk or loss
more than anything else. He's not yet learned that all growth
involves risk. His strengths are devotion, stamina, and patience.
He knows that timing is important and he will calmly wait until
the perfect moment before acting. He may appear passive or
weak, but that is usually not the case, although he is not im-
mune to being tedious. If you get him on board with your
goals, he is, of all the knights, the most reliable for a long-term
project.

The Queens

More than any other Court card, the Queens seem most likely to actually want to (and are able to) help you. They have the disposition as well as the wisdom, experience, and power to do so. The Queen's power is not always external or obvious. Like an iceberg, her influences are hidden, deep, and powerful. Although inclined to be helpful, Queens are not pushovers. They are usually busy, involved people, which is one reason they are such great resources. They can also be tricky because they are so complex. Personal connection is important for them. If they take an instant liking to you, that's fabulous; just don't betray their trust. If they decide they don't care for you, it'll be hard to change that opinion. Solidify your connection or overcome a rift with common sense, such as recognizing her skills and experience. If she decides to connect with you, she can be a friend, a mentor, a cheerleader, or a role model.

Queen of Wands

The Queen of Wands is strong and confident and is excellent at inspiring others. Call on her if you need a pep talk. She will try to encourage your own boldness or push you into taking action, whether you are ready for such steps or not. Because of her strong character, it will be hard for you to determine if she is pushing too hard or just hard enough. Know this: if she is involved in the situation, it is because it furthers her own agenda, whether that is simply empowering all of her friends or something else.

Queen of Cups

The Queen of Cups thrives on deep, personal relationships. She is usually emotionally involved or invested in her friends in a healthy way. She feels, senses, or intuits a lot and, almost always, her conclusions can be trusted. Her guidance can be invaluable. She is generally supportive and helpful and, if she has the funds or access to funds, loves to play the role of patroness. If you aren't into touchy-feely BFF connections, you may find her a little cloying but if you need a hug and some gentle empathy, go see her immediately.

Queen of Swords

If you need your résumé updated, your wedding plans organized into a spreadsheet, or a surefire approach to dealing with your boss from hell, the Queen of Swords is your hero. She's smart and experienced. Even though she's tasted the good and the bad, she's not bitter or cynical. She also has killer discernment and can sniff out deception a mile away, as well as sort out the most tangled knot to find the truth at the center. She is not above crafting a plan that both solves your problem and furthers her own agenda.

Queen of Pentacles

When you need to make the most of a little, when you need to create a blockbuster with a shoestring budget, the Queen of Pentacles can help. She may not be as elaborate as the Queen of Cups, as elegant as the Queen of Swords, or as fast as the Queen of Wands, but all the details that actually matter will be attended to and all the resources will be used to their fullest potential. From managing your budget to accessorizing an outfit, from deciding on a vacation to selecting a retirement plan, this queen is a font of useful ideas.

The Kings

In a reading, Kings represent someone with authority who will affect the outcome of the situation. Kings make decisions, delegate, and have responsibility for individuals and/or groups. They usually have achieved some level of mastery, expertise, and accomplishment and are often concerned with maintaining the status quo. They may make final decisions about hiring, scholarships, loans, or insurance coverage, actions that could have a huge impact on someone's life. Because of their roles, Kings are the least accessible of all the Court cards. Gaining their attention isn't easy. When you do have it, you have to make the most of that opportunity. Sometimes that opportunity may not be in person, but on paper, such as through a résumé or formal proposal or application.

King of Wands

The King of Wands loves business, particularly entrepreneurship or self-starters. He responds to passionate presentations and exciting, daring ideas. To influence him or gain his support on a project, point out how the plan will further his own goals, engage his passion, or use his energy and/or resources in an exciting way. He does not respond as well to emotional pleas, excruciatingly reasoned arguments, or bottom lines. Spark his creative and energetic interest, and you will have his attention. However, his attention will be short-lived, so make the most of it.

King of Cups

The King of Cups follows his heart and is moved by the hearts of others. He very much wants to do what is right. Although sensitive and compassionate, he is not a pushover. He always feels his responsibility keenly. To enlist his support and influence his decisions, appeal to his sense of tolerance and the greater good. Discover what matters to him, what ideals guide his decisions. Emotions move him, but he is mature and experienced. Childish, emotional outbursts will not serve you well with him. Balance your emotional appeal with wisdom and practicality.

King of Swords

The King of Swords worships at the shrines of reason and logic. He delights in truth, enjoys communication, and finds comfort in clearly defined rules. He is driven by the conviction that he is doing what is right. If you talk or write to him, don't bother with emotional approaches. Don't expect excitement or passion to sway him. Focus on reason and logic, have all your points clearly defined, and express them as simply as possible. He is more apt to be impressed with predicating future performance based on past performance rather than some ground-breaking new idea … unless you have a lot of data to back it up.

King of Pentacles

The King of Pentacles is practical and values results. He likes things to run efficiently and effectively while producing something of quality. Gaining his interest or support is easy. Simply show him how an idea will make his life easier or more productive. Focus on both the bottom line and good quality, and you'll find him an attentive listener. Don't bother with emotional pleas or fancy presentations...unless they are of the "form follows function" variety, in which case, he'll be even more impressed.

Playtime

Understanding and Improving Relations

Think about an interaction with someone that you've had recently that could have gone better than it did. Select a Court card that best represents you and your role in that situation. Select another that represents the other person and their role. Place them next to each other. First, notice the visual tableau they create. How are the figures in the cards relating to each other? Second, using the card interpretations in this chapter, determine what caused the conflict at a basic, symbolic level (not the specifics of the situation). Third, use what you learned from the visual and interpretive comparisons to create a scene that would have worked more smoothly.

Plan for Success

Do the same exercise, but for an upcoming interaction. Think about how that interaction would normally play out. Then, using what you can learn from the cards, create a new plan that will bring about a more harmonious conversation.

CHAPTER 7

The Major Arcana

A lot of tarot books put the interpretations for the Major Arcana first. In other books I have, too. For this one, though, I wanted to ease into the cards, showing you how they relate to real life. The Majors, as we tarot folks like to call them, are a little different. They are called "major" for a reason: because they represent not only big events but big, complex ideas. Sometimes they are referred to as archetypes; although that is not technically correct, they do represent archetypal energy. Just because they are big and important, don't get nervous about them. If you've been doing the playtime activities, you've probably already interacted with some of them. Plus, we already looked at some keywords for each of them.

Here's what you need to know about the Majors: they are doorways into vast wisdom. Do not expect to "master" them right away. Even I, after more than twenty years of hanging out with them, am still learning their secrets. Continuing to learn about the Majors is an ongoing education in spirituality and philosophy. Sometimes, after years of looking at a particular card, I suddenly see something that I've never seen before. As we grow, we move deeper into the worlds these magical doors open. In this chapter, I'll repeat the keywords that you first read about in the chart in Chapter 2 so that you have all the information in one place.

The first paragraph after the keywords will tell that card's part in the Fool's Journey. The Fool's Journey was, as far as I know, first written about by Eden Grey, who wrote tarot books in the 1960s and 1970s and is considered the grandmother of modern tarot interpretation. Her idea is that the Fool is on a journey through all the rest of the Major Arcana and is on a quest for spiritual enlightenment. If you're familiar with Joseph Campbell's concept of the Hero's Journey, this is similar.

The second paragraph helps extrapolate the Fool's Journey ideas and makes them more personal and relevant to your readings. But remember, the words and ideas given here are just the starting point, just a tiny peek into the vast and wondrous meanings, messages, and gifts that you will find in the cards as you explore on your own.

0 · The Fool

Keywords: Beginnings, innocence, freedom, spontaneity, adventure, youth, idealism, faith, purity, fearlessness, carelessness, eccentricity, folly, foolishness, stupidity, negligence, distraction, naivety, recklessness, risk-taking

Once upon a time, a young man put on his favorite clothes (all of them at once!) and started on a journey. He took a small bag of essential items, or at least what he thought of as essential. His faithful dog followed along, even though she wasn't convinced that this was a great idea. Guided by an inner drive that he couldn't really explain, he started off and although he didn't know exactly where he was going, he walked with confidence because he trusted that inner voice. The white rose he carried reminded him of his pure intentions. The red feather in his cap was a sign of his passion and commitment to the quest.

We humans love to know what to expect. It makes us feel safe. Most of the time, we can figure out or find out what is going to happen (using great tools like tarot or the Internet). The thing is, sometimes we aren't supposed to know. This "not knowing" comes up in a few cards because it is part of life's journey. When the Fool shows up, you know that even if you don't know what lies ahead, you do know what direction to go. You are just going to have to trust yourself, trust your inner voice (or your dog), and the Universe. You may not know where you are going but you will be headed in the right direction. One step at a time!

I • The Magician

Keywords: Will, talent, skill, creativity, manifestation, communication, magic, action, awareness, power, resourcefulness,
concentration, eloquence, trickery, manipulation, deceit, con,
liar, misuse of gifts

The young man, our Fool, met a great and powerful man who
could do amazing things. So the Fool made himself comfortable
and watched and learned about magic. The key is to understand
the energies that swirl around all the time. The energies have

different names depending on who is talking about them. Fire, Water, Air, and Earth. Will, Emotions, Thoughts, and Matter. Once you understand how these work, alone and in combination, you can learn to control and to manifest dreams and create reality. More importantly, though, it is necessary to control these energies within yourself. To change yourself, that is the true magic.

"You can achieve whatever you desire" is a popular belief these days and has been for a few decades. In my experience, this is not always true (and sometimes that's a good thing because we humans can be pretty short-sighted). But sometimes it is true. Sometimes you have the right idea at the right time with the right skills and resources at hand to make what you want happen. When the Magician comes up in a reading, it is a sign that this is one of those times. The first step is to be very clear about what you want. Then assess the resources you have. Then get creative. The solution may seem like a miracle, but you can make it happen.

II · The High Priestess

Keywords: Secrets, initiation, mystery, silence, wisdom, understanding, intuition, insight, subconscious, unrevealed future,
shallow knowledge, hidden agendas, inappropriate passion,
conceit

The Fool was all amped up after his visit with the Magician and
wandered around in a bit of a stupor. The calm, cool terrace of
the High Priestess was very inviting, so he rested there awhile.
She didn't really say anything, so he got bored but was too tired

to move on. So he continued to sit. At first the strange symbols around her baffled him, but he kept staring at them, wondering what they could mean. He asked, but the High Priestess wouldn't answer. He quit trying to figure it out and finally found himself lost in her gaze. She may have been surrounded in symbols, but her eyes were gateways to the undefined, indescribable mysteries of life. In the shade, he might have dozed, might have dreamed, he wasn't sure. When he decided to move on, he felt different. Like he knew things that he didn't know before, but he wasn't exactly sure what.

The High Priestess is one of the cards that tells us that we aren't supposed to know … at least not with our intellect. She represents an initiation. An initiation imparts wisdom through the experience itself. In preparation for an initiation, the initiate generally receives some training, has learned some life lessons, but the initiation itself is like the final exam. And it's not a take-home exam. You aren't given the questions ahead of time. It is a chance to put what you know into practice in ways that you couldn't have imagined. By entering into unknown territory, you learn about yourself and the world through direct experience. That experience will change you on a soul level. Your mind may never fully understand what happened, but you will know without a doubt that you've been changed.

III · The Empress

Keywords: Abundance, fertility, creativity, pleasure, beauty, happiness, comfort, nature, motherhood, mother, nurturing, love, pregnancy, generosity, dependence, codependence, laziness, stagnation, smothering, stubbornness, creative block, gluttony

The hours (day, years, he wasn't really sure) that the Fool spent with the High Priestess left him feeling like he was more out of his body than in his body. Plus, he was hungry. And a little homesick. He followed a trail of flowers to a strange alcove by the edge of a lake. In the middle of a field sat a rather gorgeous woman in a luxurious chair. Or maybe it was a throne. She wore a crown of stars, so she was probably a queen of something. She was kind and gave him fruit and milk and honey. She let him sleep in her chair and sang him songs that made flowers bloom and the air sing. He made her a crown of flowers and even though it wasn't as nice as her starry crown, she graciously wore it. Then she packed him a huge lunch and sent him on his way.

The Empress teaches through the parable of gardening and the cultivation of all life. Her lessons show us that through preparing the soil, carefully choosing what to plant, and nurturing the seeds, we will reap a harvest. This metaphor applies to all things in life, not just gardens. Life is a cycle, with death as part of that great dance. But here, in this card, we get to focus on Nature in all her abundant glory. Death is far away and, for the moment, there is more than enough for everyone. When you get this card in a reading, remember that. Also, take a cue from the Empress and be kind and generous. It's the right thing to do, particularly in this instance.

IV · The Emperor

Keywords: Stability, structure, power, authority, leadership, control, protection, stewardship, order, boss, fatherhood, father, ambition, reason, logic, confidence, tyranny, rigidity, inflexibility, controlling, cruelty, abuse of power, poor leadership, undisciplined

The Fool was mindlessly munching on one of the Empress's sandwiches when he wandered upon the Emperor. The Fool wished he had been paying more attention because he would have skipped this imposing character. The Emperor demanded to be shown everything in the Fool's now overfull sack. He wanted to know what kind of journey the Fool was on, how long it would last, and how he would make his provisions stretch for the entire adventure. The Fool, of course, had no answers and so the Emperor lectured him about the importance of responsibility, stewardship, and the general advisability of always having a plan. With the Emperor's guidance, he sorted his provisions so that he had enough for several days. Plus, the Fool did some odd jobs for the Emperor to earn some pocket money.

We would all love to be free spirits all the time, but it's not advisable. Most of us have responsibilities, if not to others then at least to ourselves. The Emperor shows us how rules and policies and organization help support life so that we can enjoy the things we love. Through planning ahead, we can be well-fed through the winter instead of practically starving through early spring when the first fruits and berries appear. Through being efficient, we create a surplus that allows for life beyond survival, for things like the arts and comforts. If the Emperor comes up in a reading, it is a message to be smart and make sure you are managing your resources properly. Don't be a greedy hoarder, because that inhibits the flow of resources for no good reason. Don't be irresponsible and hope that someone helps you out later. Be just right. Yeah, that can be harder than it sounds.

V · The Hierophant

Keywords: Education, teaching, learning, knowledge, conformity, tradition, institutions, group identity, values, guidance, orthodoxy, rites, blessing, status quo, social conventions, fundamentalism, repression, intolerance, fear, guilt, extremism, restriction, cults, abuse of position

If the Emperor was scary, the Hierophant was just crazy. What is up with that hat and those crazy gesticulations? Curious, the Fool joined the small group that listened to the Hierophant.

After a while, a basket was passed around and people put money in it. The Fool didn't but instead waited until everyone left and asked what the money was for. The Hierophant explained that it was to feed the poor and take care of the priests and priestesses who served the people. It was his job to help the people to live according to their beliefs, to make the right choices, and to grow spiritually. The Fool had a lot more questions and the Hierophant patiently answered them.

The Hierophant is one of the cards in tarot that gets a bad rap, mostly because a lot of people who study tarot have suffered at the hands of organized religion. People focus on the negative extreme rather than the positive. We don't do that with other cards, but the Hierophant really pushes people's buttons. The word "hierophant" means "to manifest the sacred." That means he helps spiritual ideals become actions in this world by teaching people how to live by their beliefs. He may also teach about spiritual beliefs and uphold or establish traditions, rituals, and ceremonies. When this card comes up for you, look at your beliefs and your actions. How well do they match up? In short, make sure you are walking your talk. If you're not, then maybe re-examine your talk. Maybe your ideals need an overhaul. Maybe you could use a teacher or guide to gain clarity.

VI · The Lovers

Keywords: Choices, crossroads, trust, communication, relationships, partnerships, togetherness, love, affection, sexuality, harmony, engagement, attraction, duality, separation,
disharmony, suspicion, jealousy, obsession, infidelity, fear
of commitment, loss of love

In a clearing at a fork in the Fool's path, a naked couple listened to
an angel. The angel said: "You both recognize each other as your
heart's desire. You are choosing wisely." The couple embraced

and turned to leave. As they did, a new path opened up as if by magic. Hand in hand, they walked the path, which disappeared behind them. The angel saw the Fool's astounded expression and said: "When you choose the path of your heart, it will be yours and yours alone." The Fool sat under the tree with apples, ate one, and stared at the burning tree. Part of him wanted to go back home. He looked back the way he'd come and saw plants emerging, reclaiming the route, making it impossible to follow. He decided to seek more adventures. A path revealed itself and the Fool continued on his way.

The Lovers is one of the cards that has changed a lot over the decades. It originally showed a man making a choice between two women, one blonde and the other dark. Symbolically, this represented the right choice and the wrong choice. Today, we have a pair of lovers, a symbol that is more specific but still means the same thing. A true love match is choosing the person who is right for you, who will help you become the person your soul wants to be. This is true of any choice you make. If you are honest with yourself and in touch with your spirit, all choices are made easier because your heart pulses in agreement with the one that's right for you.

VII · The Chariot

Keywords: Drive, ambition, control, direction, determination,
 success, triumph, victory, will, movement, progress, speed,
 travel, conquest, battle, lack of control, delay, opposition,
 stagnation, no direction, aggression, canceled trip, car trouble

The Fool felt pretty good about his choice, although part of him
was still anxious. All doubt vanished when he came upon the
Chariot. He never knew he wanted one until he saw it. He slowly

walked around it, admiring all the features. It was like a culmi-nation of his recent adventures. The starry canopy reminded him of the Empress's celestial crown. The strange symbol on the front was weird but clearly a reference to the union of the Lovers. The square sturdiness would have delighted the Emperor. The living sphinxes were like the Hierophant's idea of mystical beliefs alive in the world. The crescent moons were the favorite symbol of the High Priestess. He climbed in and noticed a wand...here, he thought, is the Magician. He held up the wand and thought about moving on. Slowly, creakily, the sphinxes stood up and started walking and the chariot lurched into motion.

This card advises you to take all the lessons you've learned recently and apply them to your life. If you want to move for-ward, you have to know who you are and where you want to go. At this point, you may not have much more than a strong desire, a passion, and for now, that is enough. That desire you have comes out of all that you've become, a logical conclusion of your life so far. You have acquired will (Magician), intuition (High Priestess), love (Empress), rationality (Emperor), training (Hierophant), and passion (Lovers). Take yourself out for a test drive. Get used to how you handle yourself in new situations. You may feel clunky at first, but just like driving a car or riding a bike, you'll become more elegant in time.

VIII · Strength

Keywords: Strength, gentleness, patience, compassion, healing, integration, courage, heart, control, discipline, fortitude, assurance, potency, virility, lust, instinct, ability, mastery, weakness, lack of discipline, control, or patience; overbearing, force, cowardice, fear, shyness

The Fool was so focused on steering his new chariot that he almost ran into a woman and a lion. Without thinking, only reacting to a perceived danger, the Fool jumped out and ran to

help. The woman was making shushing noises, trying to calm
the lion, and, amazingly, the lion was responding. The woman
knelt down and plucked a thorn from the lion's paw. Relieved
of pain, the lion fell heavily to the ground, and the woman continued to soothe him. Looking at the Fool, she said: "Most wild,
noble beings lash out or attack when they are in pain or afraid.
Like animals, other people, and your own glorious spirit."

It is easy to think this card is about brute force, physical
strength. Sometimes it is, but it also holds a deeper, more powerful meaning. We all have a part of us, often called our "shadow,"
that we try to ignore. But it won't be ignored and will, like a ne-
glected child, act out to get attention. It is only through loving
acceptance that this part of ourselves can be transformed and
integrated, helping us to become complete beings. When this
card comes for you, look to your fears, your angers, your shames.
Figure out how they are getting in the way of living the life you
want to live. Then, with great compassion, forgive yourself and
reclaim the parts of you that you've pushed away. Welcome them
back and you will find an inner strength that astonishes you.

IX · The Hermit

Keywords: Solitude, introspection, philosophy, meditation, withdrawal, contemplation, wisdom, guidance, seeking, mysticism, privacy, prudence, introversion, agoraphobia, ostracism, exile, paranoia, loneliness, isolation, extreme withdrawal, self-absorption, social misfit

It was getting dark and the Fool thought he should stop traveling for the night. As he was starting to set up a makeshift camp, he saw an old man with a lantern. The old man wasn't paying any attention to the Fool; instead he was very focused on the path in front of him, stepping carefully in the small pool of light the lantern created. The Fool followed him up a mountain. The Hermit finally stopped and said, "Why do you follow me? This is my light and my path. I go to the mountain to be alone and think about things." The Fool knew enough to take a hint and headed back down to his chariot, thinking, "If I had a light of my own, I could travel more easily in the dark." He fell asleep wondering how he could make a lantern.

When we are confused, we turn to others for advice. There always comes a time, though, in any dilemma, when you have to stop listening to others and make your own decision. The Hermit card marks a time of withdrawing from others. It suggests that you turn inward, think about all you've heard, read, and experienced and put it all together to create a picture of the truth as you see it. This truth will be yours and yours alone and it will light your path. Depending on how bright your light is or how thick the darkness around you is, you may only see the next step. That's okay. That's all you need to know because the even bigger lesson here is that the person you are now is not capable of the vision you are moving toward. With each step you become the person capable of a larger vision. It will be revealed as you are transformed.

X · Wheel of Fortune

Keywords: Fortune, chance, cycle of life, opportunity, destiny, fate, good luck, movement, turning point, annual event, bad luck, out of control, misfortune, failure, unexpected setback, reversal, delay

During the night, the Fool dreamt. He saw a large wheel covered in strange symbols and ridden by bizarre creatures, like some esoteric Ferris wheel. It turned slowly at first. The creature at the bottom was becoming more excited as it rose higher

and higher. The creature at the top started screaming and flailing, unable to stop its own fall. Then a huge hand came out
of nowhere and spun the wheel. All the creatures wailed and
clutched, trying not to be flung off. A voice whispered very
close to the Fool's ear: "It's easier to hold on if you stay in the
center."

The Wheel of Fortune is a game of chance, made all the
more difficult to win because it is dripping with riddles and mysteries. It has many lessons for us. The most obvious is: life is a
cycle. The only constant is change. Some of life's cycles are easy
to predict; they come and go with the regularity of the seasons.
Some seem completely random and chaotic. The most important lesson isn't about the nature of change. It is about your own
steadiness in the face of change. The more centered you are, the
less likely you are to be battered by the winds of change. When
this card appears, know that things will happen and you can't
control them, but you should see them as an opportunity to test
and strengthen your own spiritual center.

XI · Justice

Keywords: Justice, karma, cause and effect, equality, truth, responsibility, integrity, fairness, judgment, contract, legal action, lawsuit, trial, injustice, imbalance, dishonesty, hypocrisy, complications, abuse of power, red tape, bad decision

In the morning, the Fool got into his chariot, the weirdness of last night's dream still clinging to him. Soon he saw a formal-looking building with lots of pillars and steps. At the top of the steps was a woman holding a sword and a set of scales. People were on the steps, listening and watching as other people went up and pled their cases. The Fool couldn't hear what was being said, but noticed some people left in tears while others seemed happy and still others, determined. He asked a fellow observer what was going on and was told, "Oh, it's just people finding out that they have to sleep in the beds that they've made." The Fool must have looked blank because the person continued, "Some people never learn that they get what they deserve."

There are all kinds of justice. Very often the goddess of Justice is shown blindfolded, meaning that all are equal in the eyes of the law. Sadly, that ideal doesn't always play out. But the justice in this card is not blindfolded and is about a more universal kind of justice, more like we Westerners inaccurately call "karma." Here, Justice sees clearly and thoroughly. She carefully weighs the intentions of and outcomes of our actions to determine what we deserve. In Christian terms, it is the idea that you reap what you sow. In Law of Attraction terms, it means that your thoughts and actions create your future. If this card shows up, it means that whatever is going on is not random but instead is the result of actions that may have been set in motion long ago. This card means no one is going to get away with anything. It is time to pay the piper.

XII · The Hanged Man

Keywords: Reversal, letting go, sacrifice, suspension, surrender, withdrawal, restriction, crisis, delay, restraint, detachment, enlightenment, transformation, initiation, limbo, martyrdom, indecision, self-sabotage, narrow-minded, punishment, imprisonment, treason

The Fool saw a man hanging upside down in a tree. He wondered, remembering the lesson from Justice, what the man had done to deserve this when the hanging man spoke. "I know what you're thinking, and you're wrong." The hanging man explained that he chose to hang in the tree, giving his liberty as a sacrifice, as an offering. He sought enlightenment, a new way of seeing the same old world. He had been trying hard for years, studying and working, but making no progress so he decided not to give up but to give over, committing to wait as long as it took. "Sometimes," he continued, "there is nothing that you can do but wait. Just be still and quiet so you can listen." The Fool respected that and quit talking. But he stayed and watched for a while. Slowly, a halo of light started glowing behind the man's head, growing in size and brightness. The man stayed silent, eyes closed, but his face lit up with a radiant smile.

Have you ever felt like you've worked and worked and tried your best and yet you are not making any progress? The more frustrated you get, the harder you work until you have an amazing downward spiral going and are in danger of being sucked into a vicious vortex of overachieving control freakiness. The Hanged Man shows up in a reading to let you know to just cut that out. You may feel like the Universe is thwarting you, playing with you like a cat with a mouse, but it's not. It is trying to get your attention, trying to get you to calm down, to stop, to listen. There is something you are not getting and all your flailing about isn't helping. Stop what you are doing, close your eyes, and tune into the whispers of your heart. The answers you need are waiting for you to hear them.

XIII · Death

Keywords: Death, rebirth, endings, mortality, loss, change,
failure, destruction, severing ties, transitions, transformation, inexorable force, elimination, loss of hope, decay,
corruption, depression, despair, inertia, holding on

The Fool must have stayed with the Hanged Man for longer than
he thought because when he set off again the sun was setting. In
the distance he heard moaning and wailing, so he approached cau-
tiously and he was glad he did. Hiding his chariot, he scrambled

closer to a frightful scene. A king lay dead on a boulder while a skeleton walked over him. Other people were crying out, while a young girl offered flowers to the skeleton. The skeleton turned its head and looked right at the Fool with his empty eye sockets. A cold shiver shuddered through the Fool's soul and he knew without a doubt that he needed to walk with Death. Leaving behind his beloved chariot, his knapsack, and his few meager belongings, he walked with Death toward the sun fading on the horizon.

In tarot it is said that Death rarely means physical death. Instead, we see it as transformation. But even that word doesn't have the right connotations. It implies that you become something other than what you are. It implies leaving your ego behind, which is of course terrifying because in this human incarnation what are we without our ego? In yogic philosophy, they speak of liberation. You do not change into something else. You are who you've always been. Instead, you are freeing yourself, releasing everything that is not you in order to be more completely you. This is Death. Leaving behind all the stories that lie to you about who you really are. When this card shows up, you are invited to leave your baggage behind and shed the layers that hide your true soul.

XIV · Temperance

Keywords: Temperance, self-control, balance, moderation, harmony, synthesis, patience, health, combination, blending, management, unification, synergy, guides, angels, imbalance, excess, temper, one-sided relationship, irreconcilable differences, short-term focus

The Fool still felt dazed after his night with Death, as if he wasn't filling up his body properly. He almost bumped into an angel with glorious red wings who was doing magical things with goblets and liquid. The angel set down his cups and assessed the Fool. The angel saw into the Fool, all the piles of treasures scattered around and all of the empty spaces, too. The angel picked up the chalices again and held them up high. He turned to face each of the directions, speaking beautiful words to the sky. The angel poured the liquid back and forth before finally handing one chalice to the Fool, who, without question or doubt, drank it. The empty places in his soul filled up and the Fool was more fully in his body. He was more fully himself in every way. Death stripped him bare, leaving fertile soil and a few seeds. The angel watered the seeds and already they were growing.

We think of temperance as balance or moderation, and that is a good start. But Temperance, the Temperance in tarot, is much more subtle than that. It goes beyond the idea of creating a balanced life with a simple equation of equal hours of work, play, and sleep. This card presents us with an idea of balance that is more in line with nature. The natural world, after all, only experiences balance on the equinoxes, when day and night are equal. Other than those two moments, the natural world is either ebbing or flowing. Our lives are like that, too. Sometimes we need to put more time and energy into a certain area of life, which means less is left for other activities. When you get Temperance, you are reminded that instead of slavishly following a strict routine, try being more flexible. Routines are helpful and healthy, but only when they support your life, not control it. It is better to do the right things at the right time, giving extra attention to something if it is needed.

XV · The Devil

Keywords: Bondage, obsession, materialism, temptation, shadow, fear, doubt, lies, deviancy, ignorance, sexuality, hopelessness, lack of options, trapped, scapegoat, abuse, addiction, violence, evil, weakness, detachment, breaking free, reclaiming power

Feeling jaunty and revived, the Fool continued on his way with a spring in his step. The day was so bright and the air felt so good. He heard strange sounds, like a confusion of tortured moans and diabolical laughter. He did not want to follow the sound but knew he had to investigate. Finding the entrance to a cave, he went in and saw a man and woman chained together. A large demon taunted them until it saw the Fool. Suddenly, the Fool found himself chained to a pillar. His fear bubbled up from his stomach through his veins and panic coursed through every synapse in his brain. The chains became tighter and his terror worse. The demon's voice filled the Fool's mind: "You are nothing, you have learned nothing, you will never be worthy."

Have you ever sabotaged your own efforts? Made decisions you *knew* were wrong for you? Kept up a habit that was doing you no good? Heard your heart or your gut warn you about something but do it anyway? This is what makes the Devil so dangerous. It isn't a really big, scary demon, which would be super easy to recognize and run away from. It is really your own choices. No, that's not precisely true. Let's be very clear. It is really the choices that you make that are based in fear or grounded in an untrue story you told yourself. The more you indulge in the behavior or the further you follow the choice, the harder it becomes to imagine what you would look like or be without it. You come to imagine it is inherently you. Because you are the one who has put on the metaphorical devil's chains, it is only you who can remove them.

XVI · The Tower

Keywords: Sudden change, upheaval, adversity, downfall, destruction, catastrophe, misery, disaster, ruin, chaos, release,
awakening, freedom, escape, fear of change, prolonged
upheaval, obstacles, difficulties, losses, oppression, imprisonment, tyranny

The Fool was still bound in the demon's cave. He'd given up
struggling and was huddled on the ground, holding himself
and rocking back and forth. When he rocked forward, he could

see outside the mouth of the cave. He could see a tall tower on top of a hill, dark clouds gathering behind it, making the sky dark and fearsome. The storm churning overhead echoed the chaotic whispers engulfing the Fool's mind. As the energy built in the sky and in his brain, it began illuminating everything. The Fool's truth, a hard-won truth wrestled from the cold hands of Death, flashed in his mind and surged through his being. The chains fell away and on pure instinct the Fool ran out of the cave in time to see the sky split and the mighty tower turn into a pile of rubble on the hill.

We spend a lot of time in our lives building things: relationships, careers, homes, lifestyles, philosophies, religions, worldviews, prejudices, and ideals. It is in our nature to create structures that support our lives. The Emperor is all about useful, healthy structures. Sometimes, though, we outgrow our structures. Or we need to shed our structures so that we can grow, like a snake shedding its skin. Humans don't love change and so we often cling too tightly to our beloved structures long after we don't need them anymore. When that happens, the Universe often helps us out by, well, totally demolishing your tower for you. The Tower comes up in readings as a heads-up. You can take steps to free yourself, maintaining more control and inviting less crisis and chaos, or you can let nature take its course. Either way, you'll be able to rebuild a new structure that is better suited to your current life. For a while, you'll probably be mad and pouty about it, but in time you will realize that the experience was really a gift.

XVII · The Star

Keywords: Hope, faith, healing, cleansing, renewal, guidance, peace, blessing, tranquility, serenity, inspiration, optimism, happiness, promises, wishes, lack of faith, hopelessness, discouragement, feeling lost, broken dreams, dashed hopes, unfulfilled wishes, missed opportunities

The Fool was battered, bruised, and burned after his experiences in the Devil's cave and running past the exploding Tower. He had left everything behind with Death and felt lost, and—he hated to admit it—a little betrayed. Looking up at the brilliant stars in the dark sky made him feel better. One seemed so much brighter than the rest and he followed it into a clearing where a woman was pouring water into the pond and onto the ground. She approached him quietly, took his hand, and motioned for him to rest on the shore. She sang star songs and poured water over him. His wounds healed and he felt like his heart healed, too. He didn't know how to thank her, so he sang a song from his heart. She gave him a kiss on the forehead and he started on his path again, feeling more certain of his way.

Stars are rich symbols. We wish upon stars. We see stories in clusters of stars. We navigate by stars. We are comforted by their light in the darkness. All of these ideas play into how we interpret this card. When you get the Star, it promises healing, guidance, and restored faith. It is a gentle card with powerful effects. Have you ever felt so sad and lost, on the edge of tears, when someone gives you a hug and suddenly you start crying really hard and all your pain just bursts out in your sobs? The Star is like that hug. It lets you release everything. When you are empty, when your heart has space, the starlight pours in and fills you with a quiet confidence that everything will be okay. You will figure out how to tell the story of what happened in a way that makes sense. You will discover that you do know which way to go. You will be able to hear the soft pulse of your heart and the song of your soul.

XVIII · The Moon

Keywords: Secrets, illusion, deception, imagination, mystery,
subconscious, confusion, falsehoods, cycles, bewilderment,
anxiety, insecurity, dreams, nightmares, visions, psychic ability, secrets revealed, mysteries unveiled, insomnia, trouble
sleeping, irrationality, shadows, danger

Everything was going great for the Fool until clouds covered the
tiny stars. His way was lit only by the ghostly light of the Moon.
Shadows formed, making everything confusing. Water poured

onto the path, but he couldn't figure out where it came from. A lobster crawled out of the water and onto the path, looking like a horrible monster. He heard wolves howling in the distance and thought they were coming closer. He panicked and ran around bumping into stones and trees. When he stopped to catch his breath, underneath the pounding of his heart, he felt guidance rising up. Stop. Look. Listen. Listen from within. Calmer now, he realized his eyes were adjusting and he could see. The path led between two pillars and he knew that was the way to go.

The energy of the Moon can be challenging, depending on how you approach it. The light of the moon shows a world that looks very different from the daytime world. This is, of course, symbolic. The Moon indicates that things are not always what they seem. Monsters may actually be allies. Treasures may turn out to be curses. When this card shows up, it invites you to look not only closer but differently. Use your nonphysical senses … that is, use your intuition. … to get a fuller story of what is going on. Pay attention to the energy and don't make decisions based on initial impressions. Stay quiet and calm and tap into the eyes and ears of your soul. Pay attention to your dreams. The truth is there but it is hidden in the shadows.

XIX · The Sun

Keywords: Happiness, joy, fun, optimism, enthusiasm, glory,
clarity, consciousness, success, celebration, energy, vitality,
good fortune, greatness, life, ego, false impressions, delayed
happiness, depression, burnt out, overexposure, drought,
partial success, incomplete victory

By the time the Sun was high in the sky, the fearful memories of
the night before were fading and the Fool felt positively cheer-
ful. He came to a lovely field filled with flowers, including plenty

of sunflowers drinking in the warm sunlight. Then the Fool saw the strangest thing: a young child, who looked exactly like the Fool did many years ago, riding a white horse. The child even had a red feather, something that had been the Fool's trademark until he lost it during his adventures with Death. The child put the feather on the Fool's head, got off the horse, and motioned for the Fool to get on. The Fool did and the child vanished. The Fool rode up and down the field just for the joy of it for a very long time.

The Sun is a wonderful card with a simple message. For those of us who love birthdays, it is a feeling like that: like everything is wonderful and joyous and all about you. Another way to think of it: that feeling you get after it's been raining for days and finally the sun comes out. There is a fresh sense of happiness, energy, and enthusiasm. When the Sun shows up in a reading, it lets you know that no matter what is going on, you're going to feel completely awesome. One reason is because the sun is associated with life and new growth. It also represents clarity, the opposite of the confusion of the Moon. You will feel like you can see more clearly and understand everything you see. It connects you with your inner child who sees the world through the eyes of trust and wonder.

XX · Judgement

Keywords: Rebirth, renewal, rite of passage, calling, vocation, awakening, change, decision, forgiveness, redemption, absolution, judgement, doubt, forsaking vocation, ignoring a calling, avoiding change, unhealed wounds, lack of forgiveness, delay

After riding around, long and hard, laughing into the sunshine, the Fool felt like he was done and also, curiosity started tugging at him. What was just beyond that wall, the one with all the sunflowers along it? He climbed over and saw a huge cemetery that reached as far as the horizon. An angel appeared in the sky and started blowing a trumpet, although the Fool couldn't hear any sound. Some graves opened up and people, alive and shining with heavenly light, rose up and disappeared. While the Fool was puzzling out what had happened, he felt his soul rise up and a song burst from his throat. He didn't know how, but he could hear the trumpet and hear his own voice combining to make the most glorious, majestic music ever made. All the layers of the Fool's experiences began to merge. He lifted his face to the sky and sang his prayer of love and gratitude. He glimpsed the divine within him and in every bit of the world.

It would be great if we gave Judgement a new name because we modern folks have a hard time with it. We automatically think it is about being judged (and found wanting). We don't always realize that this is actually a card that marks a divine calling that invites us to leave a life that is dead and to embrace one that is full of life and love. We have the opportunity to free ourselves of whatever story or behavior is keeping us trapped in a coffin. This call can come out of nowhere and for most of us, that's how it happens. The card appears to give you a message: Listen to and follow the song of the divine (however you perceive it) and leave behind the things that keep you dead and small. You are meant for so much more.

XXI · The World

Keywords: Completion, success, perfection, achievement, accomplishment, victory, reward, unity, wholeness, fulfillment, endings and beginnings, celebration, center of attention, travel, delays, hesitations, false starts, stagnation, rut, incomplete work, lack of closure.

The cemetery vanished and the Fool stood in an empty field. Eventually all that vibrating with wonder made his legs weak and he laid down and watched the clouds against the blue sky.

As humans have done from the dawn of time, he saw pictures there that told him a beautiful story about success and completion. He fell asleep, dreaming about his adventures and wondering what would come next. When he woke, he was on a cloud and there was a portal marked by a laurel wreath. He couldn't see what was beyond it. The opening was reflective and he saw only himself. He adjusted his red feather, smiled with anticipation, and jumped through.

The World is the last card in the Major Arcana. Life is full of endings and beginnings, some small, some large, some happy, some sad. This card marks the successful completion of a cycle that likely required some great effort on your part. It is a great moment to reflect on the struggles that you overcame to get to this spot and to enjoy a sense of accomplishment. It is also a time to experience gratitude. Take some time to celebrate your achievement, and then hang on to your hat, because it won't be long before you start your next grand adventure!

Playtime

Life Events and Experiences

The Major Arcana cards represent major events in your life. Go through all the Majors and write down a life experience that you've had that corresponds to each card.

Using the Majors to Find Your Birth Cards

Birth cards are like your sun sign in astrology. They can tell you a little something about yourself, your journey in this life, your strengths and weaknesses. Birth cards come in sets and are connected numerically. You calculate your Birth cards by adding up the numbers of the month, the day, and the year of your birthday. Then reduce that number by adding its digits together. (In numerology, you "reduce" numbers by adding the digits together.) You continue to reduce the two-digit number until you get a number that is under twenty-one.

For example, my birthdate is 1-16-1963. When I add up those numbers and then reduce the two-digit number, I get 18 (1 + 16 + 19 + 63 = 99. Then, 9 + 9 = 18), which is the Moon.

Then I find its corresponding card by further reducing the number of the Birth card. In my example, my corresponding card is 9, the Hermit (because 1 + 8 = 9).

Most birthdates, when added up and reduced, will provide two cards, such as my birthday did: the Moon (18) and the Hermit (9). Some birthdays will generate three cards instead of two. For example, if your birthdate reduces to 19, then you have 19, the Sun; 10, the Wheel (because 1 + 9 = 10); and 1, the Magician (because 1 + 0 = 1). In the chart below, you will find all the possible permutations of Birth cards so you don't actually have to do all the math. Simply reduce down to the largest number possible under 21. Find that number on the chart and then you will know both (or all three) of your Birth cards.

Finding Your Set of Birth Cards

The groups are:

    10/1: Wheel of Fortune and Magician

    11/2: Justice and High Priestess

    12/3: Hanged Man and Empress

    13/4: Death and Emperor

    14/5: Temperance and Hierophant

    15/6: Devil and Lovers

    16/7: Tower and Chariot

17/8: Star and Strength

18/9: Moon and Hermit

19/10/1: Sun and Wheel and Magician

20/2: Judgement and High Priestess

21/3: World and Empress

Using the Majors to Find Your Card of the Year

Your card of the year represents the general theme of your year ahead. This can play out in both large and small ways. Knowing your card of the year can provide a lens through which to observe your experiences, looking for lessons and increased connection with the card.

Your card of the year is calculated similarly to your Birth card, except you use the current year instead of your birth year. So my numbers for the year this book is published are 1-16-2016 and reduce to 8, Strength ($1 + 16 + 20 + 16 = 53$. Then, $5 + 3 = 8$).

While we usually have pairs for our Birth cards, people generally only reduce to one card of the year. There is always debate about whether your card of the year energy starts in January of that year or on your birthday. In my opinion, it makes more sense for it to apply from birthday to birthday, but you may decide differently.

CHAPTER 8

Spreads and Extras

If you've done the activities in the earlier part of this book, then you've probably already worked with spreads a little bit. In this section, I will share two of my favorites. If you want to know more about spreads ... a lot more ... check out my book titled *Tarot Spreads: Layouts & Techniques to Empower Your Readings*. In that book, you'll learn about the visual dynamics at play in tarot spreads and spreadcrafting. There are tons of great spreads and lots of unique tips and techniques that make readings more dynamic and more powerful. For now, *this* book will give you enough to keep you busy!

You already learned one of tarot's most classic spreads, the Celtic Cross, in Chapter 4. You've also done some simple three-card readings. In addition to those, I'll share my favorite Yes/No Spread and my personal variation of another classic spread, the Horseshoe Spread.

Yes/No Spread

I learned this spread from Susyn Blair-Hunt's *Tarot Prediction and Divination*. Many tarot readers don't like answering yes/ no questions and will often rephrase such a question to make it more open-ended. As for me, I like using this spread at the beginning of a reading to get a sense of where the situation stands and the direction it is likely to go. That way, my client and I have a good understanding of the energy at play as we explore further. This spread gives more information than just a simple "yes" or "no" answer.

Shuffle your cards and lay out five cards in a horizontal row as shown:

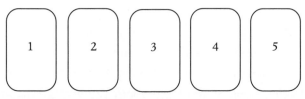

In this spread, you count cards to determine the answer. Even-numbered Minor Arcana cards and all Major Arcana cards count as "yes." Odd-numbered Minor Arcana cards and all Court cards count as "no." Because there are five cards, there will never be a tie. And, to be honest, there is rarely a complete and absolute "yes" or "no," which makes sense because the future is rarely written in stone and is usually malleable to some degree or another. So an answer could be "probably yes" or "mostly yes, but really close."

Then, after you determine the yes or no part of the reading, interpret the five cards as you would any spread. I do not use positional meanings but instead, let the cards reveal whatever message is needed.

Barbara's Modified Horseshoe Spread

This is a good, all-purpose spread that you can use in almost any situation. It is called the Horseshoe Spread because of its shape. I've modified the positions in a way that makes more sense to me and allows for the use of a really interesting technique.

The Modified Horseshoe Spread

There are a number of ways to approach interpreting this spread, which is part of its beauty. It is designed so that you can see the various energies at play in relation to each other. The technique at the end makes even further use of this integrated approach.

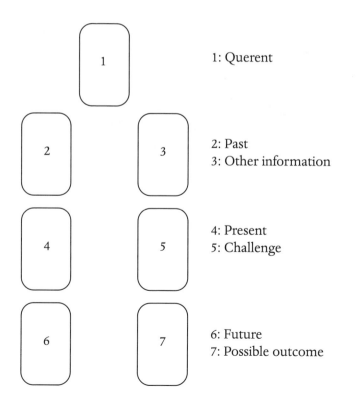

1: Querent

2: Past
3: Other information

4: Present
5: Challenge

6: Future
7: Possible outcome

Start by interpreting the spread however you normally would (hopefully this includes some of the helpful instructions from Chapter 4!), then look at the column on the left as a simple three-card past-present-future spread. After that, consider the cards across from each other in pairs: 2 and 3, 4 and 5, and 6 and 7. These pairs work together very well. Cards 2 and 3 give information about what happened in the past that is shaping the current situation. Cards 4 and 5 show the present struggles (there is usually a struggle present or a reading wouldn't be necessary, although that is not always the case). Cards 6 and 7 work together to describe the future.

For the final and, to me, really cool part, take card 1 and move it between cards 2 and 3. Observe the querent card and how its energy feels or reacts to the two cards flanking it. After that, keep moving it through the next two pairs. The significators playtime activity in Chapter 3 helped build this skill. I'd encourage you to use it because the cards in the columns describe the situation (past, present, and future), but remember that not everyone will feel or react the same in that situation. Seeing the card that represents the seeker between two cards will create a very telling and helpful story.

You now have enough spreads to at least get started. You can always invent your own spreads, too. Think about your situation and all the questions you'd like to explore. Use those questions as spread positions and lay them out in a way that makes sense to you. Yes, there are ways to improve your spread-creating skills, but you can learn a lot just by trying. Don't be afraid to make a mistake. Remember, tarot is an ever-evolving art. New practices, ideas, and discoveries hardly ever happen without a mistake or two. Also, if you don't want to buy another book (such as my

Tarot Spreads book), you can easily find tons of spreads online. Go explore! Go create!

Ethics and Mission Statement

Now that you know more than you did, review your ethics and mission statements to make sure they still reflect your beliefs. I suggest doing this once a year or whenever you feel like you've gone through a significant spiritual growth spurt.

Difficult Cards

By now you may feel like you understand most of the cards fairly well. However, there may be a few that you are still fuzzy on or ones that you just plain don't like. This is an activity I learned from one of my friends, James Wells, at a tarot conference. Decide on a situation that you want to read about. Pick a spread. Take your difficult card, and only that card, and interpret it in each of the positions. It sounds a little strange, I know, but not only will it give you a practical way to explore the many facets of a troublesome card, it will also show how the question or positional meaning helps shape the final card interpretation.

Recordings

Record your readings, even if (or perhaps especially if) you are reading for yourself. This helps you to slow down and really pay attention to what you are doing. When you listen to the recording later, you can notice (and celebrate) your strengths as well as identify and correct any weaknesses, so that you can improve as a reader. Recording while reading for yourself is great because when we read for ourselves, sometimes we lay out the cards, look at them, pretend that we've read them, and gather them up, calling it good. We don't always give as much attention to our readings as we do for other people. Give yourself the time and attention you deserve and don't rush through your own readings.

Practicing

Both beginners and long-time readers need to practice, hopefully for different reasons. Beginners want to gain confidence and experience. More seasoned readers like to try out new decks and new techniques. Here are my suggestions for getting in as much practice as possible.

Read for yourself. This has limitations, of course. Reading for yourself can be challenging simply because it is harder to be objective. Also, I don't know about you, but often I simply don't have enough questions to practice on myself that often.

Read for imaginary people. Invent a person with a short bio and a question.

Read for a fictional character. Before going to a movie, reading a chapter in a novel, or viewing the next episode of your favorite weekly TV show, do a reading to see what will happen.

Pretend a celebrity has asked for a reading and practice on them. This option may cross ethical boundaries for some, particularly those who believe that you should never read for anyone without their permission. If that is your case, then obviously this option isn't for you.

Offer free readings. In exchange for feedback, provide free readings on your favorite social networking site or join a forum or organization that allows reading exchanges.

Farewell

I could not leave you on a better note than that: practice, practice, practice! The more you engage with tarot, the more it engages with you. It will open your eyes and your mind to more than you ever imagined. When you hold a tarot deck, you hold seventy-eight keys that will lead you to the infinite possibilities of this wondrous and mysterious world we inhabit. Remember, the only rules are the ones that are rooted in your beliefs. Tarot is for everyone, for anyone who wants to explore it, but it is also always and completely your own.

To Write to the Author

If you wish to contact the author or would like more information about this book, please write to the author in care of Llewellyn Worldwide Ltd. and we will forward your request. Both the author and publisher appreciate hearing from you and learning of your enjoyment of this book and how it has helped you. Llewellyn Worldwide Ltd. cannot guarantee that every letter written to the author can be answered, but all will be forwarded. Please write to:

Barbara Moore
℅ Llewellyn Worldwide
2143 Wooddale Drive
Woodbury, MN 55125-2989

Please enclose a self-addressed stamped envelope for reply,
or $1.00 to cover costs. If outside the U.S.A., enclose
an international postal reply coupon.

Many of Llewellyn's authors have websites with additional information and resources. For more information, please visit our website at http://www.llewellyn.com.